A MANUAL OF ARCHIVAL DESCRIPTION
SECOND EDITION

A Manual of Archival Description

Second edition

**Michael Cook
and
Margaret Procter**

Gower

British Library R & D Report 5965
© British Library Board 1989

SI/G/786

Published by
Gower Publishing Company Limited
Gower House
Croft Road
Aldershot
Hants GU11 3HR
England

Gower Publishing Company
Old Post Road
Brookfield
Vermont 05036
USA

ISBN: 0 566 03634 7

Printed in Great Britain by
Billing & Sons Ltd, Worcester

Contents

Contents

Contents

Figures

Acknowledgements

A work such as this depends on the labour and cooperation of many people, acting together and singly. The project team is very conscious that it is not possible to thank or to acknowledge everyone who deserves it, and hopes that any friend and colleague whose name is wrongly omitted here will overlook the fault. We would like to record our special thanks to those whose names are given below, and we would like to acknowledge and thank the following institutions for permission to use their material:

Adam Green and the Berkshire Record Office; Jacqueline Kavanagh and the BBC Written Archives; J. P. Hudson and the British Library Department of Manuscripts; Ian Dunn, Caroline Williams and the Cheshire Record Office; Jeannine Alton and the Contemporary Scientific Archives Centre (now the National Cataloguing Unit for the Archives of Contemporary Scientists, University of Bath); Marcia Taylor and Bridget Winstanley and the ESRC Data Archive, University of Essex; Jackie Cox and Clare Clubb and the Guildhall Library Manuscripts Department, Corporation of London; Gareth Williams and the Gwynedd Archives Service; Nicholas Kingsley and the Gloucestershire Record Office; Ken Hall and the Lancashire Record Office; Andrew Griffin, India Office Records; Janet Smith and the Liverpool City Record Office; Alistair Tough and Richard Storey and the Modern Records Centre, University of Warwick; Sheila Kurtesz and the Sir John Cass Foundation Archives; Debbie Vernon and the archives service of RTZ plc; David Robinson and the staff of the Surrey Record Office;

Michael Roper, Mandy Banton and John Post and the Public Record Office; Ruth Vyse and the Barnsley Archives Service; Kath Rolph and the Tyne & Wear Archives Service; Keith Sweetmore and the West Yorkshire Archives Service and the Public Record Office of Northern Ireland. Much of the detailed work has been built up in seminar and workshop sessions, and we would like to thank once again the organizers and participants in these.

The sections on international standards have been much assisted by Hugo Stibbe (Office for Archival Descriptive Standards, National Archives of Canada); Jane Thacker (Secretary of ISO/TC9/SC9), and Ben R. Tucker (Office for Descriptive Cataloging Policy, Library of Congress).

Michael Cook
Margaret Procter
University of Liverpool
June 1989

Scope of the manual

The *Manual of Archival Description*, 2nd edition, aims to provide standards which will control the production of finding aids and finding aid systems in archival repositories and archives services. It is therefore primarily intended as a guide to normal descriptive or cataloguing practices as carried out by archivists working in general repositories.

It does not try to cater for the needs of repositories or archives services which are highly specialized, either because of the physical form of their materials (audiovisual or machine-readable archives, for example) or because of their attachment to specialized agencies (scientific research establishments for example). It is hoped that this type of archives service may however be able to use *MAD* standards and approaches to design their own systems, which will therefore not be incompatible. Outside such specialized services, archivists are accustomed to having to deal with a surprising variety of materials. It is hoped that *MAD2* will help them to do that better, more efficiently and with a better chance that their data will be more widely usable.

Neither is *MAD2* intended to be a guide for the production of bibliographical descriptions (relating to archival materials) which would form part of cooperative databases or online public access catalogues. In this respect its aims differ from those of North American colleagues who are engaged in the construction of descriptive standards for that purpose. That there is the possibility of a useful interface between *MAD* standards and those, for example, of

Hensen's *Archives, Personal Papers and Manuscripts*, or of the standards drafted by the Bureau of Canadian Archivists, is indicated by two factors:

(a) Both the North American works cited above, consciously following the model of the *Anglo-American Cataloguing Rules* (2nd edition), use the concept of the 'chief source of information', which they indicate to be 'the finding aid'. It is precisely this finding aid, a preliminary to the *AACR2*-compatible description, which is the subject of this manual.

(b) Both works, in the same way, declare or imply that they are concerned with the structure of entries in bibliographical databases.

The project team responsible for the planning of *MAD* understood from the beginning that one of their aims was the examination of the suitability of *AACR2* standards for the description of archives. In Britain, archivists had experienced little or no pressure to conform to these standards; this was in marked contrast to the situation which had developed elsewhere in the English-speaking world. Nevertheless, there was an obvious attraction in the idea of adopting a library standard, if it should prove possible. The research which led to the production of *MAD1* in 1986 has shown that the *AACR2* approach is not appropriate for the description of archives. A reading of any section of *MAD2* will demonstrate this quite clearly. The production of a finding aid system for an archives service must proceed upon quite different planning assumptions, will take a form quite different from that of a library catalogue, and will be used in a quite different way. *MAD2* has been based upon the findings of *MAD1*, which have been further developed.

Despite concluding that *MAD* cannot be based on *AACR2*, the project team has made strenuous efforts to emphasize their points of similarity. These have covered the use of common concepts, vocabulary, and the exploitation of areas which the two standards have in common. Several of the special formats come into this category. *MAD2* also includes an outline for a UK MARC format, which is an adaptation of the US/MARC AMC format. This is a specialized electronic exchange format adopted in the USA specifically for Archives and Manuscripts Control, and it has been endorsed by the Society of American Archivists on behalf of the archival profession there. At the time of first publication in *MAD2*, the UK MARC AMC outline has not, of course, received any official endorsement either from professional organizations in archives, or from the library community and its organs. Nevertheless it is hoped that the publication of the format will lead to experiment and discussion, and to the adoption of common standards, where relevant, by the library and archives communities. (The UK MARC AMC draft format is available from the Archival Description Project, University of Liverpool.)

Readers who have studied *MAD1* will observe that the principles it established have been maintained in the second edition. *MAD2*, however, has been developed in nearly every direction. The rules and recommendations have been extended, and made more precise and authoritative. Important refinements have been introduced. An example of such a refinement is the establishment of nationally operative level numbering for the various levels of arrangement and description (Section 4). In most cases additions and alterations to the standards of *MAD1* have been introduced as a result of consultations with archivists, both individually in experimental projects, and collectively in various kinds of professional meetings.

Organization of the manual

The manual is divided into five parts.

Part I lays down general principles about the nature of archival descriptions and the problems involved in writing them. One of the most obvious things about archival descriptions is that they will not easily submit to any standard of uniformity, in the sense of laying down rigid norms. The aim of this part is to encourage compatibility between different traditions of archival description by supporting the general acceptance of basic principles and a central core of common practice. This part will be mainly useful in the context of first-entry training, but all first-time users are recommended to begin by reading it.

Part II contains a table of the data elements occurring in archival descriptions. The 82 individual data elements are divided into two sectors, 7 areas and 24 sub-areas, thus allowing the data elements to be used in connected groups.

In designing the table of elements, and in particular in allocating technical terms to its parts, the project team has had regard to earlier traditions of descriptive work, including that embodied in *AACR2*. As a general rule, *MAD2* always tries to assimilate terminology and points of practice derived from the traditions of sister bodies in the information professions, wherever these seem appropriate. Accordingly, the seven areas of the data elements table may be compared with the 11 areas of *AACR2*. There are other similarities and parallels.

In Part III we show how the data elements, grouped into their areas and sub-areas, may be put together to make archival descriptions. Models are provided which are appropriate to descriptions at the various levels of arrangement.

This Part is subdivided into two. The first of these gives models for description at the principal levels: management groups (level 1), groups and subgroups (level 2), classes (level 3), items (level 4) and pieces (level 5). The second gives guidance on how to combine descriptions in various ways. Models are provided for the most usual combinations: group/subgroup (level 2, 2.nn); group/subgroup/class (levels 2, 3); class/item (levels 3, 4); item/piece (levels 4, 5); and three-level combined lists (levels 2, 3, 4 or 3, 4, 5).

Part IV consists of a typology of archival descriptions, in which the rules and recommendations of *MAD2* are illustrated. Examples from actual practice are used wherever possible. The principal models for description and the main ways in which these are combined with each other, are illustrated in this part. It is recognized, though, that in real life many different situations will occur. Procedures to meet these will have to be devised by the archivists working on the task, using the general rules and the principles which underlie these specific models.

Part V contains the special formats. These are models for writing descriptions of archival materials which have a special character. The special formats which are given in Part V are designed primarily for use in general archival repositories, and not in specialized repositories devoted to technological records. The specialist manuals which exist for sound, film, machine-readable and cartographical archives will therefore still be needed for specialized work.

There are two kinds of special formats. The first consists of material which is traditional in form, and is special only in that it exists in very large quantities in many large repositories, and can be listed or described in ways specific to itself. The two formats of this kind which are included in *MAD2* are letters/correspondence and title deeds. In drawing up standard formats for these, the project team has again had regard to the considerable amount of earlier work done by major repositories and cataloguing pioneers.

The second kind of special format is of archival materials which are quite different in technical ways or in their physical make-up, from traditional paper-based material. This category includes photographs, cartographic material, audiovisual media (including those with moving images), and machine-readable archives.

The full version of this part also has an outline format for the description of archival material using a version of MARC AMC.

The MARC AMC format is provided as a theoretical outline for bibliographical description of archival items which are to be considered for inclusion in UK MARC databases. At the time of writing (autumn 1989) there is no inter-repository database using MARC which contains archival data. However internationally there are several large databases which include archival entries. It was therefore considered useful to establish the general outline of a suitable MARC format against future eventualities. The UK MARC AMC draft format is not published with the rest of the *MAD* standards, but may be obtained from the Archival Description Project.

An appendix contains a dictionary of essential technical terms. It is one of the purposes of *MAD2* that an agreed vocabulary should be established. It has been difficult to find agreement among professionals and even between published glossaries and dictionaries, but the terminology of *MAD2* has been carefully considered, in the light of its philosophy and analysis, and does form part of the standard proposed.

The second appendix is a bibliography, limited to works directly referred to or specifically relevant to questions of descriptive standards.

PART I
THE NATURE OF ARCHIVAL DESCRIPTION

1

What are archives?

1.1 There has been much discussion of this question, particularly on the point as to whether there is a significant difference between archives and collections of manuscripts. The view taken in this manual is that there is a distinction between these, but that it is significant for descriptive purposes only in extreme cases. The extremes are represented by the following two models:

1.1A The *Public Archives Service*: This is typified in Britain by the Public Record Office. In this tradition archives are managed by a department of the organization which created the records. Few or no materials other than those created by the governing organization are taken into the system, and the main effort of the archives staff is to manage the accrual of new material coming in to existing classes, or into new classes created by the originating departments. An important part of the service's retrieval of information or of documents may be for officials in the employing body, who require the data or materials for administrative reference.

1.1B The *Historical Manuscripts Library*: In Britain this is typified by the British Library Department of Manuscripts. Here the materials are acquired by purchase, gift or bequest from sources external to the library. The materials acquired are appraised, in order to ensure that they deal with appropriate subjects, but do not otherwise have any common history. In many cases the materials accepted are likely to be individual items (such as parchments or volumes) without an organic relationship with any generative system. Users of these materials are mainly members of the public, whose purpose is to conduct research.

1.2 In practice, most archives services combine these traditions to some extent. A common situation is one where accruals of archives are received from several sources. These include the employing organization, but archives (sometimes with periodic accruals) are also received from outside organizations (archival responsibilities being delegated); the archives of defunct bodies are conserved; and manuscripts which are of relevance to the repository's interests are collected. The local authority record offices in Britain generally follow this mixed tradition.

1.3 The practices and traditions of the two extreme cases are brought closer together by two factors. Firstly, both are concerned with the acquisition, conservation and exploitation of materials important to particular fields of study. Both the public archives services and the manuscripts departments of national libraries and museums are necessary parts of the overall information resources of the nation. Each is complementary to the other, and to other collections of archives or manuscripts held in non-national, local or private institutions.

1.4 The second factor which brings the two extreme cases together is the fact, empirically observed, that the materials held in each of the two kinds of institution are rarely entirely without some of the characteristics of materials sought for by the other. In a public archives service, for instance, many of the materials received will have some of the characteristics of collections of manuscripts. Archives received as accruals from a record-generating department may be technical reports (capable of being described under biblio-graphical rules), or even collected manuscript materials.

1.5 In the same way, manuscript collections acquired by a library may display archival characteristics: the papers generated by an individual or by an organization may be acquired as a whole by the library. Such materials have the most important characteristic of archives in that they have been generated by a single system, and were transferred to the archives service as a whole in order that they should be conserved and used within a self-explanatory context. Even though the nature of this transfer may be by purchase, gift or rescue, one may still say that archival responsibilities have been delegated to the new custodian.

1.6 Because there is likely in practice to be no very clear-cut distinction between the two traditions, the view of this manual is that a standard for describing archives should begin by seeking to cover the needs of public archives services, but also go as far as possible towards covering those of manuscript libraries. Where the recommendations of this manual cease to be applicable, it should be possible to apply the rules of bibliographical description.

1.7 In-house manuals of instruction will still be necessary, to ensure that the principles and models indicated in *MAD2* may be successfully applied to meet the needs and specific practices of particular archives services.

2

Archival arrangement

2.1 The arrangement of archives is an essential feature of their management. This is true of the physical arrangement of materials on the shelves, but it is also true that arrangement is an important part of the intellectual management of the information contained in the materials. It is this intellectual management, or control, with which archival description is mainly concerned.

2.2 It is an important professional duty of an archivist to provide for what Sir Hilary Jenkinson called the 'moral defence' of the archives. This means that the arrangement of an archival accumulation should be based upon an analysis of the structure and methods of the originating organization and should display an understanding of the functions of different parts of the accumulation, in their relation to each other.

2.3 This understanding is achieved by studying and recording the original system by which the archives were generated. The archival materials may then be arranged, as far as possible, so as to preserve the original system. Beyond this brief statement, this manual does not deal with the subject area of archival arrangement, but it is necessary to remember that this process of analysis and reconstruction is also an essential part of the final system for retrieval of information and exploitation of the archive. The arrangement of archives is an essential preliminary to their description.

2.4 Archival arrangement is often formalized by the use of a classification scheme. The use of these schemes is briefly discussed in a later section of *MAD2*, but the question of classification in itself lies outside the scope of this manual, and it is therefore not considered in detail (See Section 9.9).

3

The function of a finding aid system

3.1 The theory of finding aids can be simply stated. The original materials can themselves only be arranged physically in one particular order, and this should normally be the order which demonstrates or preserves the system which brought them into being. However, users who wish to gain access to the information held in the materials need to have some way of assessing how that information might relate to their subject enquiries. The finding aids which help them to do this in effect allow the archives to be scanned in different and various alternative orders. This is the more necessary since users cannot normally scan the original materials themselves, which are boxed and shelved in closed storage.

3.2 Archival description, therefore, is aimed at setting out the various possible arrangements of the materials, which are alternative to the original structural order. By writing down essential descriptive facts about the originals, the archivist is able to create a set of representations, which can in a sense stand in for the originals, and can be set out, arranged and classified in any number of different ways. In information theory, these descriptive substitutes are known collectively as the *Representation File* or *Files*. In real life, representation files in an archival repository are components of a complex finding aid system, in which the individual finding aids take the form of catalogues, lists, inventories, calendars or guides. These are backed up and linked together by retrieval aids such as indexes.

3.3 In effect the creation of one or more representation files enables the material to be arranged in an equivalent number of different ways. However, if descriptions are really going to act as substitutes for the originals, then it is important to ensure that they are effective representations. Moreover, different representations are needed for different purposes. There is a general rule, therefore, that an archival description should contain, as far as possible, just those elements of information which are required for the purposes of a particular representation, and should omit data which is not needed in that particular context.

3.4 The main difficulty in writing archival descriptions lies therefore in determining the nature and identifying the function of the representation file(s), and applying the planned system successfully to the special character of the archives in question, to the needs of the users and of the archives service itself.

3.5 Different types of representation files are needed to carry out different functions. Some are to provide administrative control of the material, some to provide intellectual control of the information based in them. Consequently, there may be many representation files used by an archives service. Ideally, they should be combined in a single finding aid system, which may be defined as a set of different representation files designed to control the management and use of an archival accumulation. The general principle is that within one archives service there should normally be a finding aid system which consists of the following:

- a *principal representation file* containing descriptions in structural order (i.e. a list of any set of archives in an order which demonstrates the original system);
- *secondary representation files* for administrative control;
- *secondary representation files* in subject order;
- *retrieval aids* such as instructions to users and indexes;
- *specialized representation files* to control processing and to describe technically distinct materials.

Rules and recommendations for the design of finding aid systems, and for fitting together different types of finding aid are given in Sections 5–8.

3.6 The principal representation file, then, should ordinarily be in a structural form; that is, it should demonstrate the archival relationships between the components of the archive: this provides moral defence for the archive.

It is not easy to define clearly the phrase 'archival relationships', although it is one in constant use among archivists. Archival relationships are those links between components of an accumulation of archives which either demonstrate the original system under which the documents were generated, or an arrangement which was imposed upon them by subsequent administrative or business use. The term suggests that there is a distinction between this (archival) arrangement and any other, arbitrary, one (such as alphabetical or chronological order) which might be imposed by a librarian or user at some later stage. A finding aid in structural form and covering the contents of a complete archival accumulation should in principle be written at more than one level, and may be called a catalogue (especially when there is also an index).

The main representation file may take other forms. An assembly of *macro* (defined in Section 5) descriptions (usually, but not necessarily, of group, subgroup, class) may be put together to form a guide to the contents of a repository. Such a guide may also be a structural description, based on the archival relationships of the originals.

3.7 Other representations, usually containing simpler descriptions, may be arranged and used as management tools for the control of the archives considered as physical objects forming the stock of the archives service.

3.8 Secondary or additional representation files, as well as other retrieval aids, may be arranged and presented in ways that promote subject access. These may be termed subject-based, as opposed to structural, finding aids.

Further examination of the objectives and function of finding aids appears in Section 9.4.

3.9 Indexes are retrieval aids which provide access points into the representation files, so that users can find out where to begin their search for information. Normally any representation file which contains free text should be indexed. Indexes to different files may sometimes be merged into a union index, but there are many difficulties in achieving this, and it is difficult to recommend it without qualification. Merged indexes may be an important element in an integrated finding aid system. Indexing is a complex activity on which there is a considerable literature. This manual does not deal with the principles and problems involved.

Further consideration of indexing appears in Sections 9.5 and 9.8. See also the rule of representation, Section 8.4.

4

Levels of archival description

LEVEL OF DESCRIPTION

4.1 Archival material must always be managed, and therefore
described, at more than one level (the multi-level rule): see Section
5. This is not necessarily true of library collections of manuscript
material, so that this feature of archival description is one which
causes the most misunderstanding between archivists, museum
curators and librarians.

4.2 It follows from this that the units of description, where
archives are concerned, are usually collectivities. The cataloguing
units analogous to books in libraries are groups, subgroups, or
classes (all of which are collectivities), as well as items or pieces
(which are unitary).

4.3 There may be many levels of archival arrangement, and hence
of description. There must always be a minimum of two. Four levels
are normally needed to provide satisfactory finding aids to the
holdings of a repository, and there is a strong possibility that at least
two more will be needed in some cases. There is no limit, in
principle, to the number of levels which may be used. Figure 1
illustrates some possible levels of arrangement.

4.4 On the other hand, size is not a criterion for establishing levels
of archival arrangement. Consequently, although the higher levels,
such as group, normally represent very large accumulations of

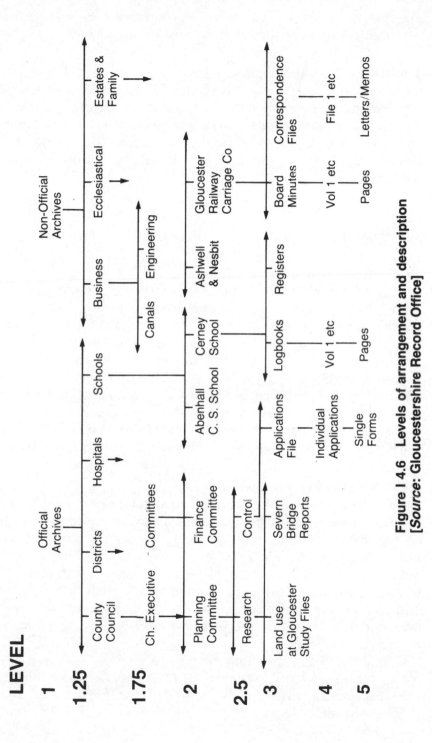

Figure I 4.6 Levels of arrangement and description [*Source*: Gloucestershire Record Office]

material, there are also cases where groups are very small. At the extreme, a group can sometimes consist of only one item.

4.5 To establish the nomenclature of these levels, a definition of the terms used is given in this section. The sources used for this terminology are detailed in the bibliography. In practice, it may be less confusing to use numbers to denote levels, than to use terminology which may seem over-complex. The numeration of the main levels is intended to be standard, so that descriptions may be readily interchanged.

4.6 LEVELS

4.6A   Level O: Repository
The highest level is that of the *Repository*. Any system of multi-repository finding aids, or national registration, or simply data exchange, must provide for a repository identification. Comparable cooperative finding aids in use among museums and libraries already include a system of codes for this purpose. However in the following analysis the repository level is treated separately since, although it should appear in the heading of archival descriptions, there is no need to take decisions about it in relation to sets of archives being arranged or described within the repository.

This level is numbered 0.

4.6B   Level 1: Management group
Within the repository, the number and structure of the levels to be used in the case of any particular archive may be decided in the light of the nature of the materials being processed, together with management needs. Within a repository, the main categories of holdings are usually treated as divisions of archival level: for example, county record offices often divide their holdings into Official, Private and Ecclesiastical archives. These and similar divisions then constitute the broadest level for management and description purposes.

Groupings of this kind may be termed *management levels*. The use of the term 'record group' in the USA may be compared.

Management levels are numbered 1.

Management levels may have subordinate sublevels, numbered as 1.nn (1 + decimal fraction).

Divisions of the holdings of a repository below level 1 may be considered 'real' (as opposed to conceptual), because they are based on actual physical accumulations of archive material, and not upon some perceived likeness between the creating agencies, or upon management convenience.

Figure I 4.6 illustrates the use of management levels in a repository.

4.6C   Level 2: Group

4.6C1   The group is the largest body of organizationally-related records established on the basis of provenance: the archives of a distinct organization, body or individual. This is level 2.

4.6C2   In manuscript libraries, and in archives services which receive significant quantities of material from exterior sources by purchase or on deposit, the term *collection* has in the past been used for a similar body of archives. 'Collection' should now be restricted to cases where there is an artificial gathering together of manuscripts from diverse sources, which are to be treated as a group.

In Canada this level is termed *fonds* or *fonds d'archives*.

4.6C3   The term 'group' does not relate directly to the size of the archive holding concerned. In the Public Record Office, groups broadly coincide with the archives of Ministries or Departments, and so are usually very large. In other repositories, groups or collections may be large or small. The essential point is that a group is an assembly of archival entities which belong together because they were generated by a body with a distinct character and a certain degree of autonomy.

Subject to any levels established for repository management (level 1), the group/collection is the principal level of archival description, and is the basic entity for purposes of management and description.

4.6C4   Group descriptions covering the holdings of a repository may be regarded as forming a separate file from descriptions at lower levels. This is because frequent changes in the administrative structure of creating organizations have loosened the connexion between groups and classes. The file of group/subgroup descriptions may then be regarded as a form of authority file governing elements in the descriptions of classes and below. If this separation between group and class level is effected, the repository must make sure that adequate cross-reference exists.

4.6C5 Repositories should have a rule about how to establish group levels in relation to the totality of their holdings. It is important that when all arrangement has been done, descriptions of the *archives of all distinct record-creating entities should be set at level 2*. This allocation of level refers to (a) the distinctness or autonomy of the body which created the archives; and (b) the presence of these archives, or a part of them, within the repository. It does not relate to political or administrative hierarchies or levels of dependency among outside bodies.

In this way, within a county, the district councils are held to rank as groups (level 2) in their own right, in the same way as major functional units within the county council itself. The district councils are not administrative dependencies of the county council, even though they may exercise fewer powers, and may in some circumstances be subject to oversight by the county. In this situation, the recommended procedure is to arrange the groups as follows:

Level 2	County Departments
Level 2	District Council A
2.5	District A Departments
Level 2	District Council B
Level 2	Town Council
Level 2	Parish Council etc...

4.6D   Level 2.5: Subgroup
4.6D1   The subgroup is a body of related records within a group, usually consisting of the records of a subordinate administrative unit, or of a functional division within the creating organization, or simply of a function distinguishable from others represented in the material.

4.6D2   Subgroups are numbered by using decimals to indicate values between 2.001 and 2.999. This device allows a virtually indefinite number of levels of subgroups (subgroups of subgroups, in effect) to be inserted at levels below that of the group. Since subgroups are always dependent on the group they belong to, interchange of data will occur at level 2, with decimals of 2 appended.

4.6D3   Subgroups are in principle natural divisions within groups. Groups may also be divided into subgroups for purposes of repository management. Where this is done, the subgroups are subdivisions of a group, established by archivists as a result of analysis, enabling the group to be broken up into manageable smaller units. Subgroups therefore should serve this purpose, that is, they should be convenient in size wherever possible. However, ideally subgroups are 'natural': they should represent the archives of distinct organizational divisions of the originating organization, or distinct functions which can be distinguished in the materials.

4.6D4   Where administrative subdivisions did not exist in the originating body, an analysis may reveal that different functions can still be identified. This is particularly useful in the case of the archives of a private individual. An individual might very probably have had functions or activities in several different spheres of life, or in connexion with different projects: these may be made the basis of subgroups in arranging that individual's papers.

4.6D5   It is sometimes possible to confuse subgroups and classes, especially in the case of smaller archival accumulations. The principle is that subgroups are based upon an analysis of the originating organization (or the various aspects reflected in the life of a person) and the different functions documented in the archive; whereas classes are based upon a physical likeness or character, derived from the way they were created and used in the originating system.

In past practice, subgroups and classes have often been merged, especially where a particular group has been managed at less than four levels. This is not good practice. If difficult cases arise, it is better to leave the subgroup level unused, and use class as the main description level.

4.6D6   Since the analysis of original structures is of the essence of archival description, it is suggested that subgroups should generally be picked out in the text of group descriptions, with their own headings or side-headings. In some cases subgroup descriptions are present but are buried within the text of group descriptions, without separate headings.

4.6D7   The group and subgroup levels are intimately linked, since the functions represented in subgroups are interlinked in the activities of the originator. It is observed that subgroup descriptions nearly always appear at some point within the text of the relevant group description, or else closely appended to it.

4.6E   Level 3: Class

4.6E1   The class (internationally known as 'series') is a set of documents which result from the same original compiling or filing process, are of broadly similar physical shape and informational content, and are referred to collectively by a specific title. Class level descriptions are numbered 3.

4.6E2   In manuscript libraries, for practical purposes, a moderately-sized assembly of items gathered together because they are of a common character may be taken as a class.

4.6E3   More generally, there are occasions where composite classes may be permitted. This is where a group or subgroup consists mainly of individual items or very small classes without strong distinguishing characteristics. In this kind of case, it may be convenient to divide the items into composite classes, each consisting of items of reasonably like character. The practice is not encouraged, but is permitted where otherwise it would be difficult to find an intermediate grouping for the materials which would assist management. Notwithstanding this provision, it is always permissible to leave the class level empty if the original material lacks it.

4.6E4   Classes may be divided into subclasses if the physical character of the class, as determined by the original system, suggests it. An example might be the case where a filing system has developed a specialized subsystem based on a single set of files, especially where this subsystem appears at a particular date and is reabsorbed into the parent class at another date.
    Figure IV.8.1 (p. 161) illustrates a subclass description.

4.6F   Level 4: Item
4.6F1   The item is the basic physical unit which is used in the handling, storage and retrieval of archives.

4.6F2   Normally, an item has an easily recognizable physical integrity. For example, bundles, files, volumes or rolls are clearly items because they are physically appropriate for handling. A practical definition might be that items are the units which are produced for reference in the searchroom.

4.6F3   There may be some difficulty in determining whether to set descriptions at level 4 or at level 5 (4.6G). Sometimes item level descriptions are determined by repository practice, as when a decision has been made to take the physical unit as the box, bundle or container as the basis for listing within a group. *MAD* has recommendations on this practice, but where it is adopted, item level descriptions will be box or bundle lists.

In other cases, item descriptions may be used to represent an intermediate stage in the levels. If this is done, item descriptions will form headnotes to piece descriptions. Alternatively, level 4 may be omitted. There should be agreement on policy in this regard, since the interchange of data at levels 4 and 5 may be significant in inter-repository schemes.

4.6F4   Where a class consists only of individual documents, and the box or bundle is not used as a unit of description, this level may be omitted.

4.6G   Level 5: Piece
4.6G1   Pieces are the indivisible individual documents which make up any archival entity.

4.6G2   When pieces are components of items, it may be useful or necessary to describe these separately. Thus a volume contains separate folios, gatherings or pages; a file contains separate sheets or pages; a box (where this is the item) contains many files, bundles or loose papers, etc. Some of these may themselves contain individual components: a box may hold a set of booklets or folders, each containing papers or pages.

Pieces within pieces are theoretically subpieces, but this ugly term may perhaps be avoided in practice by using appropriate traditional terms such as page, folio, folder, etc.

4.6G3   Where items are not physically integrated units (as when the item is a box, bundle or folder of otherwise loose papers), piece descriptions may replace item descriptions. In this case, level 4 would be left empty. See the discussion on this in 4.6F3.

The principle which distinguishes these levels is derived from the experience of public archives services, and it is not always simple to decide how to translate the terminology and practice to the circumstances of smaller and non-official archives systems. These systems should use distinct levels of description wherever they are appropriate, that is wherever their material has archival characteristics.

5

The multi-level rule

5.1 An archival description should contain at least *two* levels, a macro and a micro.

5.2 Archival descriptions should normally be written at two or more levels. Planning decisions must therefore be made to decide which levels should be used, how they should be distinguished, and how they should be combined in the final finding aid. Macro descriptions *govern* related micro descriptions, by giving information on background, context and provenance, together with information which applies to the whole of the governed materials.

5.3 When completed, a finding aid must contain macro and micro components. Either of these may contain more than one level. Generally, macro descriptions are at group, subgroup or class level, and micro descriptions are at item or piece level. However, whether a description may be seen as macro or micro is entirely relative: an item description may act as the macro component of a finding aid comprising mainly piece descriptions, for example. Similarly, sets of group or class descriptions are micro in relation to management group or group descriptions.

5.4 *Macro descriptions* have the following characteristics:

   (a)   they describe the archival entity as a whole, and do not deal with it on a one-by-one basis;

(b) they include all common or overall information relating to the entity covered;

(c) they provide one of the instruments for the management of the archives within the repository;

(d) they allow users to isolate relevant groups, subgroups or classes within which items or pieces may be searched for.

5.5 Information which is common to the different parts of an archive should be given at the highest possible level of description (the macro description), and not repeated in the lower levels (the micro descriptions).

   If this rule is neglected, redundancy usually results.

5.6 *Micro descriptions* deal with those components of the archival entity which are governed by a macro description, on a one-after-another basis. They may serve to identify specific items or pieces for production to users, or to direct users to the whereabouts of specific finding aids.

5.7 Descriptions of related archives at different levels are frequently combined in one catalogue, but each level should always be distinguished from others, preferably by writing the appropriate level numbers in the left or right margin.

5.8 Common information in the macro description may be set out for the direction of the user in a headnote, explaining the structure of the descriptions which follow. Alternatively, macro descriptions may appear as title pages to micro descriptions which follow (Section 6).

5.9 Large and complex archival accumulations will tend to require description at four or more levels. Most commonly these are group, subgroup, class and item and/or piece levels, but other combinations are possible. Additional levels may be inserted below each of these. Where this is done, level numbers using decimals are used to distinguish one from another.

5.10 Small and simple archival entities will normally need description at two or more levels. Even an archival entity consisting of only one document in principle needs a two-level description. In this case, the macro description would treat the piece as a class or as a group. The micro description would deal with it as an item or piece and would contain more detailed information. The macro description may be set out as a title page before the micro description, or as a headnote above it.

5.11 However, it is sometimes permissible to omit the micro descriptions, and to give only the macro ones, where it is desired to give users a broad overview of holdings, without a detailed or specific aspect. In principle, it is never acceptable to provide micro descriptions without appropriate macro descriptions to govern them. This is because the macro descriptions provide information on background, context and provenance which is required for the moral defence of the archives.

5.12 Multi-level descriptions of the same archival entity, or parts thereof, should be cross-referred where necessary. However, good organization of the material will reduce the need for many cross-references. It is preferable that cross-references should not be inserted into text in great numbers; they may be placed in separate fields or spaces on the page. Cross-references may also be made by the use of information in headnotes. Multi-level descriptions may share an indexing system.

An assembly of descriptions of different archives at the same level, or range of levels, may need cross-references to the appropriate micro descriptions. These descriptions too may share an indexing system.

6

Fitting levels together: headnotes and title pages

6.1 Finding aid systems are made up by combining sets of descriptions at different levels, but cross-relating. The different format of each level may make this difficult in some cases, and certainly introduces an important difficulty when computerization is in view. Retrieval aids should be provided to give additional access points.

6.2 Group, subgroup and class descriptions relating to the same archive accumulation are usually closely related to each other. A normal arrangement of these descriptions is:

Level
2   Group
2.5 Subgroups at end of main text
3   Classes in structural order

This would be a customary arrangement in a *guide* to the holdings of an archives service where sets of descriptions at levels 2 and 3 are combined horizontally (see Figure IV.3.3). The whole gives an overview of the general holdings of the repository, or of a significant part of it.

6.3 Similarly a *catalogue* is a set of descriptions which relate to a single area of the holdings of a repository, usually a group/collection with its components, but also often the contents of a management group (level 1). The catalogue brings together related descriptions at levels down from the group as far as the item or piece; again with an index to bring it together. This is a vertical combination.

6.4 Descriptions may be combined by cross-referring between separate files. If this treatment is decided on, macro descriptions form authority files.

Thus at the Public Record Office, descriptions at levels 2 and 3 are given in the *Guide to the Contents of the Public Record Office* or in the *Current Guide*, while the lists of files which constitute their level 4 and 5 descriptions, are either published as *Lists and Indexes* or, as is usual in most repositories, typescript lists are bound or filed and placed on the shelves of the Reference Room. Where this is done, the headnote to the item list takes the form of an introduction at the beginning of the list, or of a short entry at the top of the first page.

6.5 Alternatively, descriptions may be combined within the same finding aid using the relevant macro description as a *headnote*. Thus a group description may serve as the headnote to a series of class descriptions. More usually, a class description may be used as the headnote to an item description. In fact, since any description must have a reference heading which places it in context, some sort of headnote of this kind is normally essential.

6.6 It is possible – indeed usual – for more than two levels of description to appear on the same page. Where this happens, the headnote to the lowest level may be an entry within a sequence which is itself governed by a macro description. Thus there might be a sequence of descriptions like this:

level 2.5   Subgroup description
level 3   Class within the subgroup
level 4   Item within the class
level 3   Another class
            etc.

There are models for headnotes at any level. (For rules and examples see Section 15.14.)

6.7 Another way of linking macro and micro descriptions is by means of a title page or title page section.

The principal function of a title page is to display the identity statement (usually the title) of an archival entity, together with other useful information. This may amount to the whole of a macro description, thus forming a reasoned introduction to the micro descriptions which form the bulk of the data. Title page sections are expanded title pages, where extensive textual entries follow the macro title.

6.9 A title page section may be followed by a list of contents of the descriptions which follow.

6.10 Writing the level numbers against each entry, in the left or right margin but in distinctive form, is a powerful help to analysis.

7

The two modes of archival description

7.1 Archival descriptions fall into two broad types, based upon the way in which they are laid out. The two different styles of layout are called *modes*. Descriptions at any level may belong either to the *paragraph mode* or to the *list mode*.

Examples are given in Part IV.

7.2 Finding aids in *list mode* consist of tabulated columns, in which the entries for any individual level appear arranged under the field heading in columns, each entry occupying column spaces horizontally across the page. This mode can only usefully be employed when the main text entry or entries (typically in central columns) is relatively short. There is no formal limit to the length of textual entries in list mode fields, but the need to limit tabulated margins to left and right will determine the practical limitations of this mode.

List mode descriptions may include entries at different levels, the macros governing the micros. Where this is done, level distinctions are indicated by setting the left and right margins: the macro descriptions will have wider margins than the micro descriptions which depend on them.

Examples are in Part IV.

7.3 Finding aids in *paragraph mode* consist mainly of free text entries written out consecutively down the page, like numbered paragraphs in a book or report. This style is clearly to be preferred wherever text of several lines is to be entered for any field.

Although paragraph mode is quite normal for group descriptions, it can be used also for any level. The important consideration is the presence of long text or the desire to use the whole width of the page.

7.4   The mode which is chosen for any particular finding aid should remain constant throughout. To change from one mode to another within one finding aid is not recommended, although it is permissible to use a paragraph mode macro description as headnote to cover a list mode micro set of descriptions.

7.5   Very commonly, descriptions at group, subgroup and class levels are set out in paragraph mode. Rules are in Sections 10,11, and 15.9.

7.5A   Description at group level is customarily based upon a free text administrative and custodial history, together with a content and character note. Subgroups may be defined within this administrative and custodial history, but may have a secondary free text history of their own, which gives some general description of the physical nature of the materials. Examples are in Part IV.

7.5B   Classes are normally described in a free text summary: this is the content and character area, in which the bulkiest element is the abstract. This may be accompanied by specific information (size of holding, physical format, dates) in dedicated fields which figure somewhat more prominently.

7.6   In the same way, descriptions at item or piece level are commonly set out in list mode.

In particular, items or pieces are often described in tabulated lists containing three or more fields.

7.7   Despite these common patterns, finding aids which employ list mode for group, subgroup or class descriptions, and paragraph mode for item or piece descriptions are to be found. The mode chosen should correspond to the objective of the finding aid and the quantity of free text to be entered, and is not determined by the level of description being used.

7.8   The kinds of information used in descriptions at each level are described in more detail in Sections 15.8–13.

8

Depth of description

8.1 It is important that there should be a standard in each repository governing the depth of description to be accorded to archival holdings. In deciding this, regard must be had to several factors.

8.2 Depth of description must be determined, in the first place, by the *aims* of the office's finding aid system, or the *objective* of the listing work in hand. The next most important factor is the type of documentary material that is to be dealt with (special formats demand appropriate treatment). After this, the main determining factor is that of the *resources* available: resources of space, staff, time and skill. Since these, and the relative pressure of work waiting to be done, must always vary, it will never be possible to lay down absolute standards.

8.3 Preliminary or bulk listing
8.3A Repositories which use a system of double listing (an initial preliminary list, followed in due course by a final description) may aim to produce a brief summary list based upon a rapid initial analysis. *MAD* does not offer models for preliminary listing, but recommends none the less that analysis into levels be carried out, and level numbers written in the margin against the first line of the entry in any particular description. It should be possible to see to which levels preliminary (or bulk) lists are intended to belong.

8.4 RULES GOVERNING DEPTH OF DESCRIPTION

8.4A The rule of representation:

Every description should be able to serve its purpose as a representation of the original it refers to.

30

8.4A1 Descriptions are representations of the original documents, or sets of documents, on which they are based. These representations have been made in order to carry out some purpose for which the original was not available. See the principle of the representation file, Section 3.

8.4A2 In most cases, archival descriptions are 'general-purpose' representations which have been created in order to facilitate access to the materials for undifferentiated classes of users. In other cases, they can be specialized finding aids. These will include a means of accessing all the material relevant to a specialist purpose and are directed to a special class of users. At the same time they will contain some explanation as to how the particular finding aids relate to the general finding aid system.

8.4A3 The representation should always be adequate for its purpose; that is, users should be able to identify which material they wish to see, by reading the finding aid.

8.4A4 Various refinements of this purpose are possible. Users at a distance, who are not able to order up the originals, may be able to use published representations for some of their purposes. Very full representations, in the form of calendars or transcripts, may be able to replace their originals – in this case the representation file is a surrogate file. The exact fullness of the representation required is a matter of repository planning.

8.4A5 Other purposes may be administrative. For example, repository management may demand that there should be a shelf list, or location register, in order that a stock check can be done, or particular materials found. A shelf list should probably only contain such data elements as reference code, title, size/bulk and location. This information is enough to provide a representation which is adequate for its purpose, and more detail would only get in the way.

8.4B **The rule of information retrieval:**

Descriptions should contain in their text all the keywords needed in order to provide retrieval in the circumstances envisaged for this representation.

8.4B1 Keywords, in this sense, are the terms which could be used in a search, either manual or by automatic means.

Keywords may be written into narrative text fields, or they may appear in dedicated fields provided for them in the finding aid design.

8.4B2 The range and accuracy of searches possible may be improved if an index vocabulary or thesaurus has been provided.

8.4C   The rule against bias:

Descriptions should accurately reflect the actual content, meaning or significance of the original they represent.

8.4C1   It is possible for a description to misrepresent the original it refers to. This is sometimes because old and inappropriate finding aids are still in use, but there are also examples where a bias has been introduced as a result of poor planning of recent finding aids.

8.4C2   The possibility of bias arising from inappropriate description must always exist. Representations cannot normally be full replicas of the original, but must be designed to contain only the data most relevant to the immediate purpose of the representation file (8.4A). Even though they may suit the immediate purposes of the control or retrieval system, representations can only be partial portraits of the original. If the features selected for inclusion are an accurate reflection of the original in the circumstances, the portrait is in effect a good one. In other cases, the data elements highlighted may correspond to currently fashionable topics. In any case, however good the likeness is, it is effective only in the context it was designed for.

8.4C3   Bias may be introduced because the description offered is too brief, or because it is too full. Description may be made at an inappropriate level, or at an insufficient number of levels. In particular, details appropriate to micro descriptions may introduce a bias when put into macro descriptions, because they will generate keywords for index or search which overweigh terms relating to what are genuinely the dominant subjects.

8.4C4   Bias may also be the result of inappropriate data elements being selected for inclusion. It may be possible to use the headnote to explain policy on choice of data items, particularly where a particular kind of user is in mind.

Writing in place-names which are appendant to personal names in title deeds, for example, might result in clogging the place-name index. Similarly, to write in the places of domicile of witnesses in title deeds might give a bias to descriptions or retrieval aids based on topographical holdings.

Again, in Quarter Sessions rolls, more index entries might be made for cases of riot than for other events. Without a covering explanation, this might give a bias to the final description, by suggesting that questions of riot occupied the business of the court in some special way.

8.4C5 Bias may also be the result of a lack of uniformity in the description of different parts of the repository's holdings. If there has been a variation in the depth of description accorded to later accessions, because of lack of resources, then users may not be certain what reliance to place on the finding aids, or they may give a misplaced reliance on them.

Further investigation of this subject is required in order to provide more detailed standards.

9

Other aspects of archival description

9.0 As well as level and depth, at least eleven other aspects of description should be considered when designing a finding aid system.

9.1   The variety and uniqueness of archival materials.
9.2   The size and complexity of the originating organization.
9.3   The accrual of new material to existing classes.
9.4   The purpose and design of finding aid systems.
9.5   Access points into the finding aid system.
9.6   Retrieval strategies by users.
9.7   The variety of terminology used.
9.8   Indexing.
9.9   Classification systems.
9.10   Reference coding.
9.11   The relationship with national or international cataloguing rules or systems for bibliographic description.

9.1 The variety and uniqueness of archival materials

9.1A It is notorious that each archive accumulation has a character of its own, and that this character impresses itself on the form and content of its finding aids. Archivists are often advised to allow the archive to speak for itself in shaping the descriptive material.

9.1B At the same time, the describer's independence in allowing this self-expression of the archive has been circumscribed in two directions. The repository usually tries to lay down a *house style* which determines at least the general appearance of the resulting lists; and the examples in Part IV show that in practice most archive accumulations are particular instances of broad groups or categories of archive types. Even where there is no guidance from house styles, archivists try to follow *pre-established patterns* or classification schemes wherever possible.

9.1C The aim, then, is to allow an archive accumulation to impose its own special character upon the descriptions based on it, while at the same time

   (a)   conforming to house-styles and standards; and
   (b)   conforming to appropriate general models.

9.1D MAD standards are aimed to provide a model which, while remaining sufficiently flexible to allow a proper response to the needs of specific archives, allows the interchange of data between repositories with a minimum of adjustment. Archivists faced with the problem of constructing a finding aid system for the management of an unusually individual archival entity are encouraged to apply MAD standards and principles as far as possible. If this is found to be impossible they are asked to communicate the problem to the Archival Description Project.

9.2 The size and complexity of the originating organization

9.2A The size and complexity of the originating organization is an important factor in the design of finding aids. A large and complex organization produces archives which will need to be arranged in several levels. These levels have to be combined, and retrieval aids provided, to bring the components of the finding aid system together. At the other extreme are relatively simple archival entities such as the private papers of an individual.

9.2B Neither size nor complexity affects the analysis of a set of archives into levels of arrangement. It is possible to meet groups which consist of few items, or even of only one. Subject to the multi-level rule (Section 5), any appropriate level of description may be used or omitted in any particular case.

9.2C The design of databases, and of rules for house styles must allow for this diversity of structure. *MAD* gives models for different circumstances, but it will always be necessary to adapt these to local and specific conditions.

9.2D Changes in the administrative structure of the creating agency may affect the way in which accruals are managed: see Section 9.3.

9.3 The accrual of new material to existing classes

9.3A The ability to manage accruals to existing classes is central to archive administration.

It is of course a question mainly for archives services which manage materials accruing from continuing bodies, such as government departments, and can therefore best be illustrated by practice in large repositories attached directly to an administration. However, even manuscript libraries can experience the phenomenon of an archive accumulation which arrives in two or more successive deposits, and sometimes in a series of deposits which are likely to recur an indefinite number of times.

9.3B Some archival entities have received accruals in the past which have affected their structure, but further accruals are not expected. In general it is good practice to *retain the arrangement determined by the originating system, including the divisions which may have been introduced by deposit in two or more accruals.* However there may be cases in which this would create unnecessary anomalies, and where it would seem desirable to *restore an underlying original arrangement.*

9.3C Administrative change over time causes problems in the management of later accruals. When an archive-generating function is transferred from one administrative department to another, the archive service must inevitably make a decision about how to deal with new accruals of archives relating to that function. Such accruals must either be *added to the original class or they must be treated as a new class.*

If the former choice is adopted, an anomaly will arise, for the later sections of the relevant class will appear to be in the 'wrong' group: archives will be listed under the general heading of a department which did not in fact have any responsibility for their creation. If the latter choice is taken, the continuing records of a particular function will be broken up into sections not necessarily readily understood by users, and divided among different groups.

9.3D Solutions to the problems of accruals belong mainly to the area of archival management rather than that of archival description, though obviously the solution adopted will have an effect on the finding aids and means of access. Successful assimilation of new accruals depends on the design of the levels of arrangement and description.

9.3E   A repeated sequence of new accruals to a class will tend to produce unnaturally long classes, and therefore unwieldy finding aids. Where there are frequent accruals, the resulting lists will have amended sections which may be numerous. The prospect of constant new additions will make it difficult to provide an accurate overview, or macro description, and at item level some way will have to be found of incorporating new lists. Users may have to consult different annual sections or appendices to the list. Cross-indexing will be made difficult, and complex referencing may be needed.

It is difficult to suggest a way in which these difficulties could be avoided. Periodical reassessments, resulting in newly-written macro descriptions, may perhaps be possible. This suggestion reinforces a general recommendation that published finding aids need to be revised from time to time.

9.3F   Where later accruals to a class have been restructured or re-referenced by an organization which has taken them over before their transfer to the archives, then, in general, it would be preferable to *retain the later structure and references*. A full description would include a note of obsolete reference codes, which may refer to a section of the administrative history of the group or subgroup.

9.3G   If there are to be accruals to the archives of a superseded body, this body should be treated as a group or major subgroup.

9.3H   In all cases, the macro description should make the accrual status clear to the searcher by entries in the administrative and custodial history sub-areas.

9.3I   Where there are gaps in sequences of archives, reference codes indicating the missing entities should be provided in square brackets.

9.3J   Where later accruals must be interposed within a numbered sequence, subnumbers should be used. Generally, this problem will be mitigated if reference codes are numbered in sequences which are confined to specific levels or sections. See Section 9.10I.

9.3K It is recommended that in repositories where there are regular accruals to groups and/or classes, descriptions at group, subgroup and class level should be processed and stored separately from descriptions at item and piece level (with suitable cross-references). The macro descriptions may then be regarded as a form of authority file governing the micro descriptions.

9.4 The purpose and design of finding aid systems

9.4A A finding aid system may contain both structural and subject-based finding aids. Structural finding aids will always be regarded as primary by archivists, and will normally constitute the main representation file, because they provide for the moral defence of archives.

Structural lists, however, may not be regarded by users as the most immediately useful, and in extreme cases it may even be necessary to provide specific programmes of user education to make them intelligible. Subject-oriented finding aids do not give moral defence of the archives but may be more immediately usable to inexpert readers.

9.4B Subject to the principle of moral defence, in cases of doubt, the requirements of users should be taken as the guiding principle in the planning of a finding aid system.

9.4C The aim in establishing a finding aid system is to ensure that each finding aid has an objective complementary to the objectives of each of the other finding aids.

9.4D An integrated finding aid system will contain such elements as:

- a *guide to holdings*, arranged in management groups (level 1), and containing sets of descriptions at group and subgroup level (2);
- sets of *class descriptions* (level 3), associated with their groups;
- sets of *item descriptions* (level 4), arranged under the class headings they belong to;
- descriptions of components of single groups, lower levels arranged under the appropriate higher descriptions;
- indexes and instruction sheets to allow the user easy access.

9.4E There are two broad categories of finding aids, those whose objective is *administrative control* (the management of the physical processes, including retrieval), and those concerned with *intellectual control* (the management of the information contained in the material).

9.4F There are also finding aids constructed mainly or entirely for the use of staff within the archives service (in-house finding aids: an

40

example would be a location list or shelf register), and those intended mainly for use by external readers.

9.4G As a general principle, finding aids intended for access by users should be regarded as published material. Wherever possible, this publication should be formal, making use of legal deposit and cataloguing-in-publication (CIP) facilities. Where this is not possible, de facto publication may be achieved by making the finding aids available to users in the searchroom, and by distributing copies to the National Register of Archives, and to appropriate reference points (such as public or academic libraries) elsewhere.

9.4H Finding aids intended only for in-house use are not subject to the requirement of publication. The degree of confidentiality to be accorded to in-house finding aids is of course a matter for decision by the repository itself.

9.4I The practice of constructing multi-repository finding aids is growing, and is likely to become more general as national information systems develop. Finding aids should be designed to facilitate cooperative publication. The *MAD* standards are intended for this purpose.

9.4J Recommendations and rules for combining sets of descriptions, given in Section 15, should be followed.

9.5 Access points to the finding aid system

9.5A Every finding aid system has access points. These are the points at which any user, whether internal (repository staff or staff of the employing agency) or external (academic or member of the public), begins a search for relevant material. It is desirable that the finding aid system should be planned in such a way that suitable access points are presented to the user, and lead to successful retrieval paths.

In *AACR2*, access points are entries in dedicated fields which can be extracted in turn and put at the head of a bibliographic description. The function of access points within an archival finding aid is somewhat different, since the single-level set of descriptions is not a practical model. Instead, access points should be regarded as entries within fields or within records at different levels, which can be identified for retrieval by some searching process, and which will lead the user from one level of description to another.

9.5B Initial entry to a finding aid system may be from the top or from the bottom of the finding aid system.

9.5C Entry from the top occurs when users begin with the macro descriptions and proceed to the micro, or from the less detailed to the more detailed. For example, they may use a guide to find which groups are likely to be of interest, and from there go to class and item lists. (Macro and micro level descriptions are explained in Section 5.)

9.5D Initial entry from the bottom is by means of an item or piece list, or by their indexes.

There are certainly many common situations where this is the most appropriate method, although in principle it is not possible unless the user has already some background knowledge which will supply the most essential information about the structure or context of the archive. This information is normally obtainable from the macro descriptions, although it may already be available to expert users from external sources. For example, family historians may be able to go direct to a particular parish register, but they will be drawing upon a store of pre-existing information about the historic boundaries of parishes, the nature of parish archives and the kind of information held in registers. In fact, a concealed initial entry always exists where a reader uses pre-existing knowledge to go straight to micro descriptions.

9.5E   There may also be initial access by way of retrieval aids, such as 'advice to users' leaflets, or indexes.

9.5F   As a general principle, finding aids which contain free text should also have an index to that text (provided that online searching is not an option). See Section 8.4B.

9.5G   In general, the question of appropriate access points should be considered when finding aid systems are designed. Planning decisions will have their effect on the shape of the lists and indexes produced.

9.6 Retrieval strategies by users

9.6A There are three principal strategies employed by users (including staff users) to identify archival documents relevant to their enquiry. These are direct identification, browsing and scanning.

9.6B *Direct identification* occurs when the user knows one or more of the identifying features of the documents sought. These can be read off, and the document ordered. In terms of the finding aids, the main requirement is that the data belonging to each entity should be clearly identifiable as belonging together. The reference code or other call number should be easily spotted and transcribed. For this to be clear, it may be necessary to repeat the full reference code for each entry.

9.6C When *browsing*, users read pages of the finding aid in order to pick up any information or ideas which strike them as useful. It would be common to employ faster reading techniques, which usually involve focusing the eyes on an imaginary vertical line down the centre of the page. Keywords which appear in the text on either side of this line can be recognized in passing. A short line and clearly printed text are helpful.

In browsing, the user's immediate retrieval objective is often not clearly defined. Free text descriptions such as those in the administrative/custodial history or the content and character areas are most suitable fields for this strategy.

9.6D When *scanning*, the user's retrieval objective is likely to be more or less clearly defined. The action of scanning is to identify specific keywords, names, character strings or references by running the eye over the finding aid until these appear. The user will rapidly identify the fields or spaces on the page on which targets are likely to appear. For this strategy, a strongly formatted page with dedicated fields will be best.

9.6E Since there is therefore some degree of conflict between the page layout and field structure most suitable for each mode of retrieval, it is important that finding aids should be formatted appropriately, so that information for scanning is separated from information for browsing. Sets of descriptions should normally be assembled on a well-designed page, in which blocks of text occupy the centre of the page, and data which can be put into dedicated fields will occupy their own spaces on the paper. Easy identification requires that each entity in the list should be clearly separate from any other.

9.6F List mode finding aids are generally more appropriate for scanning, while paragraph mode finding aids are more suitable for browsing. *MAD* formats are intended to be sufficiently flexible to allow a range of combinations, and all *MAD* layouts contain some structured areas as well as free text. (List and paragraph mode finding aids are explained in Section 7.)

9.7 The variety of terminology used

9.7A Although there is a good deal of broad agreement on the principal technical terms, there has been imprecision as to the names to be used for the different kinds of finding aid. *MAD* gives a standard definition for each term in the dictionary section.

9.7B It is recommended that those terms should be avoided which are derived from:

- library practice: e.g. catalogue (in the bibliographic sense), collection;
- foreign usages: e.g. *fonds d'archives*;
- antiquarian tradition: e.g. calendar (except where there is surrogation), repertory;
- private practice within particular institutions: e.g. schedule, register.

9.8 Indexing

9.8A   It was noted in Section 3.9 that indexes are an essential part of an archival description, and in Section 9.5D that they are necessary access points to a finding aid system. The importance of indexes in archival description (traditionally not great) has been increasing in recent years. *Indexes* should be planned, and *should be a part of an integrated finding aid system.*

9.8B   *Users should be able to employ indexes directly.*

9.8C   Indexes may be the means of initial access to descriptions at any level, but there are problems in retaining distinctions of level where indexes exist at more than one of them. There are examples of successful two-tier indexing systems, but it is recommended that *indexes to descriptions at a particular level should be kept separate from those applicable to other levels.*

9.8D   *Indexes are secondary retrieval aids.* This means that their aim is to lead users to descriptions in the finding aid system, rather than directly to original materials. It is recommended that indexes should refer to keywords within the finding aids and not to data in the originals which has not been described in the finding aids. Where the latter practice occurs, the indexes form one of the central components of the finding aid system, and are primary.

9.8E   It is recommended that *index references should be reference codes rather than page numbers*, where this can be done reasonably (e.g. it may be impractical when the system uses long reference codes).

Usually this means that long textual fields in descriptions at group level are best done by page number, while description sets at levels 3–5 tend to be more suitable for using reference codes in the index.

9.8F   It should be possible to amalgamate or merge indexes in various combinations, either manually or by translating them to a computer format. This means that the *indexes within a finding aid system should* if possible *have a common infrastructure and format.* Indexing should be based upon a coherent philosophy and upon a controlled and structured vocabulary. Distinctions of level should be maintained.

It is probably not possible to devise or adapt a common vocabulary for the whole area of archival content (as was attempted in 1977 by a working party of the Society of Archivists). The most successful thesauri are those constructed for defined in-house purposes, but the possibility of vocabularies/thesauri/ classification schemes being developed to cover technical areas cannot be discounted.

9.8G Despite what has been said, there is an influential body of opinion which regards the possibility of common infrastructures for indexes as impractical. It is clear that there is considerable scope for further research in this area. Research might include studies of local or specialized vocabularies, and the adaptation of library and museum authority lists.

The development of online search facilities may weaken the case for investment in indexing structures. In terms of standards of description, however, this technology does not appear to threaten the norms proposed in this Manual, since the principle that free text descriptions should contain all the keywords necessary for searches, is unaffected (Section 9.5D).

9.9 Classification systems

9.9A The aim of classification schemes is to improve compatibility between descriptions, and to avoid the need for archivists to duplicate analysis and research. The problem is that non-archival classification schemes are not generally suitable.

9.9B This question was raised but not discussed in Section 2.4. Although excluded from the terms of reference of the Archival Description Project, some principles have to be outlined, but there is scope for further research on the role of classification schemes in the management of archives. Some of this research to develop new schemes, which may become models for others, is in progress under the aegis of the Specialist Repositories Group of the Society of Archivists, and the Business Archives Council (1988). Findings should be incorporated into later editions of *MAD*.

9.9C Archivists should consider using existing classification schemes if a satisfactory scheme exists. There will be very few cases where there is no useful precedent or pattern which will serve to direct archivists' arrangement of the material into levels, and their arrangement of the resulting descriptions. It is often necessary however to introduce local variations into any such scheme to accommodate unique features in the archive being described.

9.9D It is important to distinguish between the different kinds of classification schemes in use. Some are based upon an analysis of functions in the originating organization, some upon the physical form of the archival materials, and some analyse certain elements in the origin or content of the archives (such as reference to manorial courts). Some classification schemes are a mixture of one or more of these elements. In some schemes different elements coincide.

> Thus, in the classic scheme for Quarter Sessions archives, developed originally in the Essex and Bedford Record Offices, there are functional divisions: the Court in Session; Enrolment, Registration and Deposit, etc. In other cases the divisions are based upon form (bundles, order books).
>
> In another commonly used scheme, that for Parish archives, categories based on function and those based on form clearly coincide – e.g. Registers.

9.9E   Classification schemes based upon subject are not suitable for the structural description of archives because they would override the arrangement derived from provenance, and introduce complications or dispersion where different subjects are dealt with in the same class. Classification schemes are only suitable for application to archives where:

(a)   the classification scheme is based upon the administrative structure and functions of the originating organization, and not upon subject;

(b)   the originating organization is one of several which have the same title, administrative structure, or general character, each organization operating in a different territory or with some other individuating characteristic;

(c)   the archive is complex enough to demand the use of a classification scheme.

Thus archival description should follow the arrangement of the material, which in turn reflects the original system which generated it. However classification schemes which are current in the library or museum communities could be used for structuring secondary finding aids, such as indexes, and may be included in future authority lists.

9.9F   There are also conventions governing the format of finding aids (particularly published finding aids) which may be termed classification schemes. Thus it is customary to arrange the management groups and group descriptions in a guide so that the official archives groups come first, followed by groups from other areas of origin – e.g. ecclesiastical, private. In general where a format convention is operating, it should be followed.

9.10   Reference coding

9.10A   Reference codes are the link between the original materials and the representations of them which are the finding aids. At the end of the process, *each archival document must have a unique reference number which will identify it.*

Archival description has no other direct interest in these reference codes, except that they should be in a form which is capable of entry into the descriptive format. This may be a problem in some cases when computerization occurs, and is always important when the format of archival descriptions affects the efficiency of retrieval.

9.10B   There are five possible objectives in designing a reference code, though it is difficult to achieve them all simultaneously.

(i)   Reference codes identify items for *retrieval*, and therefore are included in a location index.

(ii)   They identify pieces in *citation*. Since it is impossible to keep track of all citations, this requirement means that reference codes should if at all possible be permanent.

(iii)   They indicate to readers the present custodian of archival materials and suggest something of their *context*. Full codes should therefore carry an element to identify the repository.

(iv)   Reference codes may suggest a *relationship* with other groups, subgroups, classes, items or pieces; they may also give an indication of which level the cited description is dealing with. This means that there should normally be a distinct parameter within the code corresponding to each level. However, where there is a large number of levels within a group, rigid adherence to this principle may lead to errors and undue complexity in citation, or in searchroom requisitions. Simplification would be recommended in this case.

(v)   They should act as a *security* check.

Uniformity of usage will bring benefits to both users and archivists, and will help to attain security objectives.

9.10C   In some repositories an additional feature of the reference codes (derived from the classification scheme used) is a subject element, designed to allow retrieval of relevant documents following certain kinds of subject enquiry.

For example, some systems will allow the retrieval of all documents which bear upon manorial rights, or which deal with estate management. Because of the possible confusion between structural and subject elements, this practice is not recommended.

9.10D   The following example illustrates the points made above.

```
Reference code = LUA/DCU/GM1/2,p.3

Level number:  0     1   2    2.5   3   4   5
Code:              LUA  /D  CU/   GM  1/  2,  p.3

Levels
0              Repository (Liverpool University Archives)
1                  Management group (D: deposited archives)
2                  Group/collection (CU: Cunard archive)
2.5                  Subgroup (GM: General Manager's Department)
3                  Class (1: Registers)
4                      Item (volume no.2)
5                      Piece (page no.3)
```

9.10E   Description formats must be able to accommodate existing reference codes, even where these are lengthy or employ unusual alpha-numeric combinations. Codes should appear on each page or section of the description.

9.10F   Accession numbers are often used for document identification, temporarily in many cases, permanently in some. This practice is not ideal, since it abandons several of the objectives listed in Section 9.10B, and may depend on subsequent relisting taking place (Section 8.3). On the other hand, relisting may allow better analysis and a more rational permanent coding.

9.10G   The choice of letters in reference and classification codes is often based on the desire for a mnemonic system. This is only successful where there is a limited number of categories. It has been abandoned in the Public Record Office (for new classes, at least), and *MAD* recommends that mnemonic systems should not normally be sought.

9.10H   Alphabetical characters should be used for subgroup and above; and numerical characters for class and below.

This rule may be waived if excessive complexity would result, or where long-established styles cannot be varied.

9.10I *Reference codes for class descriptions and below should be numbered serially from 1 in each unit of description.* The practice of using a continuous series of numbers throughout a group is not recommended.

9.10J The problem of gaps in sequences of archival materials was discussed in the section on accrual (Section 9.3).

9.11 The relationship with national or international cataloguing rules or systems for bibliographic description

MAD attempts to reconcile standards of archival description, wherever possible, with standards operative within the library, information and museum communities. The standards, organizations and systems commented on here are the following:

AACR2	Anglo-American Cataloguing Rules, 2nd edition
APPM	Archives, Private Papers and Manuscripts, 2nd edition
ISBD	International Standard Book Description
MARC (AMC)	Machine-Readable Cataloguing (Archives and Manuscripts Control)
CCF	Common Communication Format
ISO	International Standards Organization
SGML	Standard Generalized Mark-up Language
MDA	Museum Documentation Association standards.

9.11A *Anglo-American Cataloguing Rules, 2nd edition (AACR2)*
9.11A1   In 1961 the International Federation of Library Associations and Institutions (IFLA) undertook a study of cataloguing principles which resulted in an agreed statement (the Paris Principles). Subsequent work produced the International Standard Bibliographic Description (ISBD – see below Section 9.11C) and it was within the framework of ISBD(G) that the first edition of *AACR* was published in 1967. The second edition appeared in 1978.

9.11A2   *AACR2*, prepared by a consortium of the American Library Association (ALA), British Library, the Library Association (LA), the Library of Congress (LC) and Canadian representatives, reconciles national rules with the ISBD and develops them. *AACR2* rules are now used in most English-speaking countries and have influenced many other non-Anglophone systems. Revision work is continually in progress, and is especially important, given the rapid growth of electronic and centralized cataloguing agencies and information networks. *AACR2* deals not only with printed material: it also covers cartographic materials, manuscripts, music, sound and film recordings, graphic materials, machine-readable files and three-dimensional artefacts, and there are many provisions in it which cover all types of bibliographic description. Interpretative manuals are available for many of the specialized chapters. Its general introduction states:

These rules are designed for use in the construction of catalogues and other lists in general libraries of all sizes. They are not specifically intended for specialist and archival libraries, but it is recommended that such libraries use the rules as the basis of their cataloguing and augment their provisions as necessary.

9.11A3 Within *MAD*, an attempt has been made to assimilate archival practice with that of *AACR2* wherever the two seem to coincide; similarly, the same terminology has been chosen wherever there seems to be common practice, even where this has meant a movement away from previous custom among archivists.

It is clear, however, as noted in the Introduction, that *MAD* proceeds from different basic principles from those of *AACR2*, and it has not been possible to incorporate many of the latter's general terms. In particular, it has not been possible to find a place in *MAD* for the following *AACR2* terms and concepts:

The **chief source of information.** The chief source of information is the archive itself; alternative sources of information are any other sources available. It was not thought useful to include in *MAD* any statement so general. Further discussion of this point is given in Section 9.11B.

Headings (main, additional, subject). The underlying concept which this term expresses is the keyword or entry which appears at the top of an index card, in a card catalogue, by which the card is sorted. Card indexes are not a satisfactory model for archival descriptions, and therefore the term and the concept have not been used.

Similarly, the term **access points** has been used sparingly. This term also refer to statements which appear at the top of an index card: *MAD* avoids this usage. In a more general way, access points can refer to any facility for allowing users to pick up subject references in a finding aid system, and it is in this sense that the term has been used in the Manual (Section 9.5A).

The concept of **uniform titles** is relevant to archival description, but has not been developed in a *MAD* context. This is simply because it has for the most part been absent from archival practice, and because in consequence there is no infrastructure of authorities available. Future work will be needed to remedy this defect.

9.11A4 More positively, *MAD* uses the concept of functionally grouped data elements which is an important feature of *AACR2*, together with the associated terminology. In *MAD*, data elements are grouped into seven areas, which may be contrasted with *AACR2*'s eleven areas. The content of the areas, however, is different, since most of the areas of *AACR2* are not relevant to archival materials.

9.11A5 *AACR2* standards should be considered when standards for bibliographic descriptions of archival materials are in question, for example for entry into bibliographic databases. See Section 9.11B.

9.11B Archives, Personal Papers and Manuscripts (APPM)

9.11B1 Archivists, and particularly North American archivists working within the tradition of manuscript libraries, who tried to follow Chapter 4 of *AACR2* found that the chapter on the cataloguing of manuscripts was unworkable. In the USA, Steven Hensen's *Archives, personal papers and manuscripts: a cataloging manual for archival repositories, historical societies and manuscript libraries* (*APPM*) (Library of Congress, Washington, 1983; revised 1988) was written as an improved alternative for archivists who were seeking to use an *AACR2* approach for their cataloguing. Hensen's introduction examines the structure of an *AACR2* description, and sets out the principles upon which archival description must be conducted.

In the context of North America, the use of MARC formats has become so dominant that this in itself is sufficient justification for continuing to adapt and reinforce *AACR2* rules and authorities. Much of the revised *APPM* consists of authority lists.

Hensen lists the following as the central principles of archival description:

Repositories produce complex finding aid systems; bibliographic (*APPM*) descriptions are distilled from these, and in effect finding aids are the chief source of information.

Provenance is more useful than *AACR2*'s 'statement of responsibility' as a basis for describing this aspect of a manuscript's creation. Similarly, there are different forms for date, edition, title and physical extent: in particular, there are full rules for supplying titles.

The principle of using collective entities as the cataloguing units is fully accepted, and repositories are given latitude in setting description levels.

9.11B2 These principles correspond with those of *MAD*, and therefore an attempt has been made to use as many of the terms, concepts and principles of *APPM* as possible. In some cases the wording of *APPM* rules has been incorporated, with acknowledgement. Despite this, *MAD* does not follow the structure or conventions of *APPM*, because the latter is essentially an application of *AACR2*.

Where *MAD* principles and procedures are not applicable, because the material being described is close to being bibliographic (for example, in the case of literary manuscripts), it is recommended that *APPM* standards should be adopted.

9.11B3 *APPM* contains authority lists for headings and uniform titles which could be adapted for use in a British context.

9.11B4 *APPM* is itself an authority for cataloguing rules and conventions within North American online databases. An adaptation of it could be made to supply this function in a British context.

9.11C The International Standard Bibliographic Descriptions (ISBD)
9.11C1 The ISBDs, issued under the aegis of IFLA, specify requirements for the description and identification of different types of bibliographic materials. They are intended to '... provide the maximum amount of descriptive information required in a range of different bibliographical activities', and to provide conventions for the punctuation and arrangement of data elements.

The stated primary purpose of the ISBDs '... is to aid international communication of bibliographic information ... by (i) making records from different sources interchangeable, so that records produced in one country can be easily accepted in library catalogues or other bibliographic lists in any other country; (ii) assisting in the interpretation of records across language barriers so that records produced for users of one language can be interpreted by users of other languages; and (iii) assisting in the conversion of bibliographic records to machine-readable form'.

The ISBDs are not intended for use on their own but as the basis for specific national or international cataloguing rules. Almost all countries which have produced cataloguing rules in the last 20 years have used the ISBD structures in their own codes.

9.11C2 There are ISBDs for most specific types of material and the terminology has been incorporated in the *MAD* rules for Special Formats where appropriate. However, none of the ISBDs are designed to cover anything but published material and there is at present no ISBD which deals with manuscript material. Since 1981 IFLA has had a policy of reviewing the existing ISBDs every five years. The following are the most relevant to materials which are the concern of archivists:

ISBD(G)	General principles
ISBD(A)	for Older Books (Antiquarian)
ISBD(CM)	for Cartographic Materials
ISBD(M)	for Monographic Publications
ISBD(NBM)	for Non-Book Materials
ISBD(S)	Serials
ISBD(M)	for Printed Music

9.11D Machine-Readable Cataloguing (MARC)

9.11D1 MARC is a general format for the electronic exchange of bibliographical information. There are special formats for various types of bibliographic or comparable information and pressure from bibliographic networks in the United States has led there to the development of one of these for archives: MARC AMC – the Archives and Manuscripts Control format. A UK interpretation of the MARC format was developed as part of the *MAD2* project. Copies are obtainable from the Archival Description Project.

9.11D2 MARC formats are intended solely to control the shape and character of bibliographic information which is to be exchanged between institutions as part of a machine-readable network or system. The existence and nature of MARC need not necessarily affect the cataloguing or descriptive practices which an institution does for itself.

9.11D3 The MARC AMC format was issued in 1984 by the Society of American Archivists and other interested bodies in conjunction with the Library of Congress. Following the appearance of the first edition of *APPM* in 1983, it was possible to provide an *AACR2*-like set of rules for the format of descriptive entries, and for designing appropriate fields in the record.

9.11D4 The MARC formats combine strictly defined fields with variable length text fields, distinguished by prefixing them with tags. The text fields are normally subdivided into a number of subfields, each of which is intended for a particular kind of data. These highly structured fields are an important strength of the system, for they allow the output of the data in many different forms.

However, it is often difficult for archivists to break down archival data to allocate it to appropriate fields and in-house guidelines are needed where the repository is participating in a MARC-related system.

9.11E   The Common Communication Format (CCF)
9.11E1   CCF was developed in response to the growing dangers of lack of compatibility and uniformity among national standard formats for electronic exchange of bibliographic records, with parallel exchanges occurring between formats used for library exchange and those used by abstracting and indexing services. Six existing bibliographic exchange formats were analysed to find which data elements were held in common and it is these data elements which now form the core of CCF.

9.11E2   The three major purposes for which CCF was designed are:

- To permit the exchange of bibliographic records between groups of libraries and bibliographic services;

- To permit a bibliographic agency to manipulate with a single set of computer programs bibliographic records received from both libraries and bibliographic services;

- To serve as the basis of a format for a bibliographic agency's own database.

9.11E3   Perhaps of equal relevance to archivists was the resolution to devise a standard technique '... for accommodating level, relationships, and links between bibliographic entities'. Thus the concept of the record segment was also developed, which permits a single bibliographic record to contain descriptions of more than one item. These items may exist at various bibliographic levels (and the relationship among the items described or identified are conveyed through segment linkage). In addition, within the description of one item, related fields may be linked through field linkage.

CCF conforms to ISO 2709–1981: Format for Bibliographic Information Interchange on Magnetic Tape. *CCF: The Common Communication Format* (p. 13) gives a list of eight further ISOs to which the format conforms as far as possible.

9.11F   The International Standards Organization (ISO)

9.11F1   The ISO promotes internationally accepted standards originally formulated as a response to a specific proposal from one of its member bodies, usually the national standards body (in the case of the UK this is the British Standards Institute (BSI). This proposal will have come, in turn, from any interested organization within that country which has perceived the need for a standard in a certain area. If the subject field of the proposal is acceptable to the international community of standards organizations, then the work is referred to an appropriate ISO technical committee (TC) for development.

9.11F2   The committee responsible for the standardization of information and documentation practices is TC46. Its subgroups cover a wide range of activities, including formulating guidelines for the presentation and description of documents, and standards facilitating the storage, exchange and retrieval of information.

9.11F3   ISO standards are most relevant in connexion with the transmission of data through electronic means, and therefore should best be considered in the context of MARC formats. The most significant standard is ISO 8211: Information Processing – specification for a data descriptive file for information interchange.

A selection of ISO Standards and Recommendations of interest to archivists is listed in J. B. Rhoads, *The applicability of UNISIST guidelines and ISO international standards to archives administration and records management: a RAMP study* (UNESCO, Paris, 1982). A full list of standards produced by ISO/TC46 and other technical committees can be obtained from the British Standards Institution, 2 Park Street, London W1A 2BS; Tel: 01 629 9000.

9.11G   The Standard Generalized Mark-up Language (SGML)
9.11G1   SGML is a generic coding language used for marking up texts (including machine-readable texts). Generic mark-up is not linked to any specific set of typefaces, but it can be applied to a particular typological system in order to control a final publication. This is done by analysing the structure of a document, identifying such structural elements as headings, side-headings, title page, etc., and demonstrating their role in that document. The elements so determined can be marked by tags on the original page or in a compuscript. In this way, several documents which look different on the printed page can easily be assimilated and presented in a uniform manner.

9.11G2   Generic coding has potential for the control and transfer of archival descriptions and finding aids. It is being used in some repositories, notably in the British Library's Department of Manuscripts. In this department, style sheets are prepared to control the processing of manuscript descriptions; these use tags to indicate the structure of the list. It is intended that the same tags will be used to facilitate further processing of the data.

9.11G3   Archivists should be aware of the existence and potential of SGML which became an ISO draft international standard in 1985.

9.11H   The Museum Documentation Association (MDA) standards
9.11H1   These standards are embodied in the MDA *Data definition language and data standard*, 1980, and related documents.

In some ways attempts to standardize archival description have more in common with similar efforts of museum curators than with those of librarians and information scientists. Like archivists, curators are dealing with unique objects which lie outside the scope of traditional bibliographic cataloguing. Just as some of *MAD*'s work derives from earlier work done by the Society of Archivists working parties, so much of the current MDA standards are based on work done by a curatorial working group, the Information Retrieval Group of the Museums Association (IRGMA).

9.11H2   The MDA data standard resulted from an analysis of the data elements which made up typical museum records. Throughout the development of the standard, the aim was to establish a record structure which could deal with logically related data covering many disciplines.

Historically, the structure of object descriptions was displayed on specially formatted index cards. These cards were marked with boxes corresponding to data elements. Where elements were dependent in a hierarchical system, the boxes corresponding to them could be nested. At a later stage, computerized description was introduced, the system allowing structured tables of data elements to be displayed.

The same principle has been adopted by *MAD*, with the addition of standard levels of description.

PART II
THE DATA STRUCTURE OF AN ARCHIVAL DESCRIPTION

10

The purpose of data structure in archival description

10.1 Archival descriptions are essentially structured. They are made by putting together a planned combination of recognized and labelled items of information. These items of information are *data elements*. The data elements which are to be used are selected from a list, which is given later in this Part of *MAD*.

10.2 The data elements selected are then fitted together in ways that conform to the patterns or models of archival descriptions given in Part III. When a pattern or model is put together in this way, specific information about the archival entity being described can be written in.

10.3 It is a basic principle of archival description that data element patterns should be constructed with a view to making searches as easy as possible.

A structured description which contains a set of data elements laid out in the form of one of the models for an archival description provides a useful basis for the management and retrieval of information from archives. This is because the data elements can be made to facilitate techniques for searching. This is true whether these techniques are manual (scanning, browsing), or mechanized (online search). Since particular data elements can be labelled by tags, or identified from their position on the page, searches can be concentrated on those sections of the description which are most likely to contain the information sought. Because of this, archival descriptions will normally contain an apparatus of some kind which enables each data element to be easily identified (Section 9.6).

10.4 Archival descriptions therefore are organized collections of data which are the values assigned to data elements. The data in each element is given its character by the nature of the element concerned, and may therefore be strictly controlled by the rules for that element. Despite this, most or all archival descriptions necessarily contain free text, and this in whatever mode is selected for descriptions. It is an important principle that no field in an archival description should be arbitrarily limited in length. A parallel principle is that free text should contain all necessary keywords for retrieval of the materials or the information in them (Section 8.4B).

11

How the table of data elements is made up

11.1 The table of data elements which is given below contains a list of what are considered to be all the data elements normally used in archival description. If additional data elements are needed in particular cases, these may be supplied in accordance with local practice.

11.2 The table of data elements is divided into two main sectors. The *archival description sector* contains information which is primarily for the guidance of users, and is in the public domain. The *management information sector* contains information needed for the administrative control of the archival materials and of processes within the repository, and is generally not in the public domain.

11.3 Within the sectors, data elements are grouped into *areas and sub-areas*. This is for the convenience of archivists carrying out the description process. It is assumed that when manual listing is being done, archivists will use areas or sub-areas as wholes, except in cases where there is special need for more detailed structuring. Automated descriptive systems may have distinct input fields corresponding to the data elements.

11.4 It is expected that in normal circumstances, archival descriptions will consist of entries corresponding to some of the data elements in the archival description sector. Entries within the management information sector are only needed where the repository is using *MAD* standards to control internal management in the case of the entity being described. The level at which the description is being set makes no difference to this principle.

11.5 If the archival entity being described is one of the special formats, different rules apply. For these, see Part V.

12

Summary of the table of data elements

Archival Description Sector

Identity Statement Area
    Reference code
    Title
      Term for form/type/genre
      Name element
      Span dates
    Level number

Administrative and Custodial History Area
    Administrative history
      Source of administrative authority
      Office holders/personal or corporate names
      Place of origin
      Previous administrative systems and identification
      Significant dates
    Custodial history
      Sequence of ownership
      Place of custody, sequence of location
      Method of transfer
      Date/conditions of transfer to archives
      Source references
            (See also Accession record)
    Archivist's note
      Relational complexity and status
      Appraisal principle
      System of arrangement
            (See also Arrangement record)
            (See also Appraisal review record)

Content and Character Area
  Abstract
    Date
    Site, locality or place
    Personal or corporate names
    Events, activities
    Subject keywords
  Diplomatic description
    General diplomatic: form/type/genre
    Problem features
    Predominant language
    Script
    Special features
    Secondary characteristics
  Physical description
    Physical character
    Quantity, bulk or size
        (See also Location record)
    Physical condition
        (Cross-reference to Conservation area)

Access, Publication and Reference Area
  Access record
    Access conditions
    Copying conditions
    Copyright information
        (See also Issue for use record)
  Publication record
    Citations
    Bibliographic details
  Related materials
    Related materials elsewhere
    Existence of copies
    Other finding aids
    Lists deposited elsewhere
  Exhibition record
    Circumstances
        (See also Loan record)
    Physical condition
        (See also Conservation area)

Management Information Sector

Administrative Control Information Area
Accession record
　　　　(See also Custodial history)
　Number, code, reference
　Date(s) of accession/custody
　Method of acquisition
　Immediate source
　Conditions
　Deposit agreement
　　　　(See also Location record)
　Funding
Location record
　Place of storage
　Bulk
　　　　(See also Physical description)
　Accruals
　　　　(See also Accession record)

Process Control Area
Arrangement record
　　　　(See also Archivist's note)
　Sorting method
　Funding
　Dates of completion
Description record
　Description plan
　Funding
　Dates of completion
Indexing record
　Person responsible
　System, controls used
　Funding
　Dates of completion
Issue for use record
　Access status & policy
　　　　(See also Access record)
　User's identity.
　Time, date of issue and return

71

Frequency of reference
Enquiry record
  Identity of enquirer
  Dates
Loan record
  Person/organization to whom loaned
  Dates of despatch
  Dates of return/due for return
  Insurance or security details
          (See also Exhibition record)
Appraisal review record
  Procedure used
  Action taken/recommended
  Action date
  Appraiser
          (See also Archivist's note)

Conservation Area
  Administration
          (See also Physical description)
  Conservation record
   Repairs required
   Level of priority
   Conservator responsible
   Start and finish dates
   Repairs carried out
   Recommendations for future conservation
   Materials used
   Funding
          (Cross-reference to Administrative control
          information area)

13

General rules for the table of data elements

13.1 At least one of the data elements of the identity statement is obligatory in every description. Apart from this, all data elements are optional, and may be left unused in any description.

13.2 Any data element may be selected for use at any level of description.

13.3 In many cases there may be a choice between two or more alternative areas or sub-areas, for the entry of particular data into a description. The choice is at the discretion of the archivist, but the nature of the alternatives, and wherever possible the preferred practice is indicated in the specific rules below (Section 14).

13.4 There is in principle no limit to the length of the entry corresponding to any data element in a finding aid. (Limits may of course be imposed by the requirements of local systems.)

13.5 Apart from the identity statement, areas or sub-areas may, if preferred, be treated as blocks of free text. In this case, data elements belonging to those areas or sub-areas would be incorporated within the text without necessarily being delimited in any way. This would be normal in some manually constructed descriptions.

13.6 Archivists may choose to construct their descriptions on areas or sub-areas rather than upon sets of individual data elements. It is expected that descriptions will not normally be explicitly analysed into data elements except where a system is being used which employs such an analysis in its data entry forms.

13.7 Any area, sub-area or data element may contain a cross-reference to the repository's relevant correspondence files and source references for statements made in the text.

13.8 The table of data elements is not intended for use with special formats. For each of these there are specific tables of data elements in Part V.

14

Specific rules for the use of data elements

14.0 Section 13 gives general rules for the use of the data elements. This section contains an explanation of the content of each data element, and rules for its use.

14.1 THE ARCHIVAL DESCRIPTION SECTOR

The purpose of the archival description sector is to contain information primarily of interest to the user (including internal or staff users). The data entered here is considered to be part of a description of the materials, suitable for promoting their exploitation by users. The information in this sector should be regarded as being in the public domain.

The sector has four areas:

(1) The identity statement, which identifies the archival entity being described, and gives broad initial information about it (including the level of the current description), for labelling purposes;

(2) the administrative and custodial history, which records the context, background and provenance of the archive;

(3) the content and character area summarizes the information contained in the archive, and gives information about its form; this provides the basis of a practical finding aid;

(4) the access, publication and reference area, which explains how the archive has been or may be used.

More detail is given on each of these areas and their components in the following sections.

14.2 The identity statement area

It is obligatory in any description (at whatever level) to provide at least one of the data elements of the identity statement. This element must be sufficient to establish the identity of the archival entity being described, and to allow its retrieval. Beyond this minimum, however, the area serves to allow users a means of rapid or preliminary identification of relevant materials.

14.2A *Reference code*

Rules and recommendations for the form of the reference code are given in Section 9.9.

14.2B *Title*

14.2B1 The purpose of the title sub-area is:

- to give a label which can be used in ordinary speech, or in a preliminary guide;
- to provide the equivalent of a main heading in a bibliographical finding aid;
- to direct users to more detailed descriptions.

The title should be brief and should include words which uniquely identify the materials being described.

14.2B2 The title sub-area may contain one or more of three data elements:

(i) a simple term indicating the form, type or genre of the materials;
(ii) a name element;
(iii) simple span or indicator dates.

Further details on the components of these elements follow.

14.2B3 *(i) A simple term indicating the form, type or genre of the materials*
This data element is often left unused, since it is quite normal for the user to assume the type of material from the context. For example:

At group level (2):

'Port of Preston, 1836–1899' implies
'Archives of the Port of Preston, 1836–1899'

At item level (4):

'[Minute book of] League of Nations Union 1936–1948'
'[Volume entitled] Barnes Parish Church Roll of Honour'
(See Section 14.2B4).

At class level (3), the element is normally necessary since classes are based upon a type or form of material e.g.

'Bucklow Union salary registers'.
(See Section 14.2B4)

Where this element is to be used, enter the most specific form of material that is applicable. For group or subgroup, use one of the following general terms (use other terms where appropriate):

'Papers': this means an accumulation of personal papers containing more than one kind of material, e.g.

'Papers of George, Duke of Clarence'.

'Records' or 'archives': this means the records or archives of corporate bodies or organizations, e.g.

'Russian-American Company records'.

'Collection', or 'collection of papers': any group of materials formed artificially round a person, subject or activity and which otherwise lacks integrity and unity of provenance, e.g.

'The William Smith collection of documents on local militias'.

For the description of entities larger than item, use an appropriate plural or collective form of material designation (e.g. 'letters', 'correspondence', 'diaries', 'journals', 'legal documents', etc.).

For single items such as manuscript volumes (e.g. a diary, a letter book, an account book, a ledger, etc.) and for uniform accumulations such as letters, speeches, sermons, lectures, legal or financial documents, enter the form of the material which is most specific and appropriate.

14.2B4 *(ii) The name element*

The name element in a title normally consists of, or at least contains, the name or names of one or more persons and/or corporate bodies or organizations predominantly associated with or responsible for the entity being described.

14.2B4i Choice of name element

(a) *Where there is no formal or original title*, or if the formal or original title is insufficient or misleading, a supplied title is used for the name element. Since most archival entities do not have a formal title in the bibliographic sense, the name element is usually supplied by the archivist. This element should be brief and descriptive, following a recommended terminology or name authority file if one is used.

There is often no original title for subgroups: these titles may be derived from the name of the functional division, or function, which has been the basis of their creation (e.g. Legal Department (Records), financial (records) etc.), with date or other qualifiers as necessary. Where there were no functional divisions in the originating body (as in the case of private papers), distinct functions may be inferred from the content or grouping of the items, or from extraneous sources (e.g. the papers of a scientist divided into research work, conference papers, personal papers etc.). A suitable title may then be supplied.

The title of a class should wherever possible be that given to the class while it was still in current administrative use. Where this rule cannot be applied, the title should refer to the class's distinguishing characteristic and be derived from an examination of the archive itself. Since the definition of a class is that it is a set of archives with a unifying physical characteristic, the title should normally contain terms describing the physical form of the materials in the class. Examples of typical class titles are:

> Board Minutes of Felpersham Hospital;
> Register of Adoptions, Wirral Union;
> Tate & Lyle Directors' Out-letters.

The name element of an item title is derived from one of the following:

> any title or heading written on the item;
> an inferred original title by which it might have been known when in current use;

the physical character or content of the item;
the diplomatic character of the item;
the informational content of the item.

In the absence of one of these, it is quite usual for items not to have titles but instead to have a brief abstract or statement of content. Example:

Black soft-covered notebook containing calculations in Danish and German.

(b) *Where there is a formal title*, i.e. one which was assigned by the original creator or by the original users of the material, record this title exactly. Traditional titles or titles allocated in common speech may be included as parallel titles or subtitles.

Where there is a formal title which is misleading or insufficient it should be recorded and noted as such in the content and character area. Alternatively, a supplied extension or subtitle may be used to complete or explain an insufficient formal title. Example:

St Jude's Mission [and Benevolent] Committee minutes

14.2B4ii It is intended that the name element in a title should be short and convenient to provide a satisfactory general label for, or identification of, the entity: however, there is no firm rule as to its length. A title may be expanded, or subtitles or parallel titles (as indicated in 14.2B4i) may be added if the main title is not clear and self-explanatory. In general, the name element of the title should be kept short, and additional material placed in the content and character area.

Choose names which record persons, families or organizations which are predominantly associated with or were responsible for the entity being described. If the entity consists of the papers of two or more persons or families, or if it holds the archives of two or more organizations (e.g. where one body has been taken over or replaced by another), use all of the names primarily associated with the creation of the material in the name element. Example:

Archives of the Booth Steamship Co and Booth Iquitos Line.

Record names in direct order of natural language. Names may be abbreviated if the full name appears elsewhere.

Uniform titles[1] or additions to uniform titles may be added in round brackets after the main title if this is the practice of the repository, and if there is a suitable authority list. Example:

Papers of Edward Leach (microfilm copies).

Uniform names should be used if this is repository practice, and if there is a suitable authority list. In other cases, the following general rules should be followed.

Where an individual has alternative names (e.g. titles of nobility or office), use the name by which the person is generally known, e.g. Benjamin Disraeli, not Earl of Beaconsfield; *but* Duke of Marlborough, not John Churchill.

Extended titles or full names can be given in the administrative history area or in the content and character area.

14.2B5 *(iii) Simple span or indicator dates*

The purpose of the span dates is to help the other elements in the title to give a clear immediate means of reference to the materials, not to give a precise and detailed description of content. The dates should therefore normally be restricted to simple years or spans of years, delineating broad chronological periods, or helping to identify a particular institution, or broad phases in the life of that institution.

The dates must refer to the actual period when the documents were created. If an item consists of, or includes copies of or extracts from, documents of earlier dates, these dates, if cited, should appear in the administrative and custodial history area, or the content and character area as appropriate.

If the materials deal with or refer to periods different from the period when they were created, these periods may be included in the name element of the title if they are significant for preliminary identification, or in the content and character area if they are not significant in this way but are needed to complete a true picture of the contents of the archive. Example:

Tommy Atkins's reminiscences of 1914   1936.

Enter inclusive or span dates directly following the name element or any other title information that has been added to it. Simple dates in

---

[1] Uniform title and uniform name are technical terms in *AACR2* and *APPM*. For an explanation see the Dictionary of Technical Terms.

the title may follow the name element directly (with or without a comma) or may be placed in a right-margin date column on the same line as the name element (as in the example above).

For groups, subgroups or classes, the year or years alone, singly or as a span, are normally sufficient, provided that full date information appears elsewhere. If the dates within the material are scattered, it may be preferable to give the bulk (effective or operative span) dates in the title, rather than literal extreme span dates, exact dates then appearing in the content and character note as noted above, or as text in item/piece lists. Example:

Span dates given in the class title as 1789–1809 may appear more exactly in the item/piece list as:

/1 1789 July–1795 June 3
/2 1797 June 14–1800 Feb 22
/3 1803 Jan 14–1809 May 12

[In this case, a stray document of 1750 would not necessarily be noted in the title span dates.]

For a single item or piece, give the exact date, expressed as year, month, day: e.g. 1742 May 7. If the item lacks date information or the information is incomplete and must be completed from internal evidence or an external source, enclose it in square brackets in accordance with the standard listing conventions (Section 17.6) in Part III. If the date information is incomplete and the missing components cannot be supplied, use 'undated', 'no date' or 'nd' according to local practice. If month and day information is missing, it may be omitted if there is no strong reason for giving negative information.

It is recommended that simple year dates should be given in a tabulated column at the right of the page, to facilitate scanning. Complex or lengthy dates should not be provided in the title sub-area but should be treated as text within appropriate areas.

For more examples of dates (including approximate and estimated dates) see the standard listing conventions (Section 16.6).

14.2C *Level number*
It is generally desirable that there should be a level number attached to any description. However, it would not normally be displayed in a finding aid intended for public use. (In this respect it is an exception to the other data elements within the archival description

sector. It is placed here because it forms part of the identity statement.) The purpose of the level number is to confirm and record the analysis which lies behind the arrangement of the archives being described, and to facilitate the comparison and exchange of data.

14.2D *Examples of titles:*

Level

2 DH	Papers of the first Duke of Heswall,	1801–1857
2 BO/PS	Borchester petty sessional court,	1835–1850
2.5 BO/PS/A	Borchester special sittings,	after 1840
3 BO/LA/C1	Coronation sub-committee minutes,	1937–1955
4 BO/LA/C1/3	Coronation sub-committee minute book No.3 1953	

14.3 Administrative and custodial history area

This area is intended to allow for the information needed to establish the background, context, provenance and archival history of the entity being described. It is characteristic of (but not exclusive to) higher levels of description, and is required for the moral defence of the archive.

The area contains three sub-areas, administrative history, custodial history and the archivist's note.

The first two of these are not necessarily to be treated as distinct from each other. These sub-areas may, if appropriate, be written together as connected text. Generally, information on the history of custody should come at the end of a text which deals first with the origin and then with the transmission of an archival entity.

The most recent events in custodial history (especially the circumstances of *transfer to the repository*) may be omitted here and placed in the accession record if repository management considerations require; for example, if there is need for confidentiality. Where there is no strong reason for this choice, however, the custodial history sub-area should contain information on final transfer even if a separate accession record is kept in the management information sector.

Where factual statements are made in the text of this area, it is a good practice to cite sources for them, whether these are external or internal to the materials. Administrative histories frequently include a bibliography section and/or footnotes.

14.3A *Administrative history*

This sub-area is normally treated as free text, without limitations as to length.

Record any significant information on the origin, progress, development and work of the creating organization of the archive or on the life and work of the person mainly responsible. Include all details required to explain the structure, nature or scope of the materials, as they were created and used.

For persons, the information needed usually includes dates of birth and death, place of birth, successive places of domicile, occupations or offices, information on original and maiden names or pseudonyms, significant accomplishments, place of death, etc. If such details appear in readily available and accurate published sources, (e.g. *The Dictionary of National Biography*) these can be listed and the details given in this area need not be lengthy; in the

same way, uniform names may be obtained from current authority lists if these are used.

For corporate bodies or organizations, the information may
include data on the origin, functions, purpose and development
of the body, its administrative hierarchy, and earlier, variant or
successor names. It is important to include the successive names
and offices of principal movers in the organization, since these
names are often the access points for subject searches.

Particularly important information, for which data elements are
provided, is likely to be:

- the source of administrative authority for the function documented;
- information on individuals or office-holders important in the
  formation and development of the function;
- information on place of origin;
- information on previous administrative systems, identification
  codes and the sequence of changes in these;
- significant dates for all events mentioned.

An example of a corporate administrative history

Houghton le Spring Rural Sanitary Authority was set up
under the Public Health Act 1872. The Rural District
Council, established under the Local Government Act
1894, inherited the functions of the former Rural Sanitary
Authority in 1895 when the Act came into operation.
Houghton le Spring Rural District Council was abolished
on 1 April 1937 and the area split up among the neighbouring local authorities, namely Hetton Urban District
Council (UDC), Hetton UDC, Houghton le Spring UDC,
Durham Rural District Council (RDC), Easington RDC
and Sunderland RDC.

From 1872 to 1894 the office of Clerk was discharged by a
local firm of solicitors, Messrs Smith and Jones [address].
Subsequently, the clerkship was discharged by the officers
of the RDC.

Although the Rural Sanitary Authority and the Rural
District Council were distinct local authorities, significant

---

breaks in classes do not occur at 1894 and therefore the records have been treated as one group rather than as two.

The records in this group are an amalgamation of parts of four separate accessions, as follows...

Records inherited by Houghton UDC in 1937 and later deposited at Durham Record Office. Transferred to Tyne and Wear Archives Service on 28 July 1976.

[*Source*: Tyne and Wear Archives Service]

An example of an entry relating to a person

WILLIAM HENRY STOKES, CBE, JP (1894–1977)
Trade unionist. Born in Coventry, educated in Earlsdon Primary School and night classes. Worked in engineering, served in the RAF 1918. Married Frances Beckett 1918. Involved in National Minority Movement and Communist Party (1920's–1937). Member of Steam Engine Makers Society, helped to form the Amalgamated Engineering Union, 1920. He was District President of this 1936, and convener of shop stewards at the Riley Motor Works. He became a full-time divisional organiser of AEU in 1937. During the war he joined the Midland Regional Board of the Ministry of Supply, and was chairman before he left in 1950 to join the Iron and Steel Corporation. After the winding up of the ISC in 1953, WHS toured America. He was personnel manager of Armstrong Siddeley 1954–1959, and part-time member of the East Midlands Electricity Board 1959–1964, JP 1950, and chairman of Coventry bench 1966.

Related material, oral history interview 1967, held in Coventry Polytechnic Library.

[*Source*: Modern Records Centre, University of Warwick.]

14.3B *Custodial history*
This sub-area is normally free text, without limitation as to length.

It may be combined with the administrative history sub-area, but in this case, should normally be placed at or towards the end of the main text.

Make a record of the history of the custody of the materials. Include information on:

- the sequence of ownership changes, from the original to the present owners, up to the point of transfer to the archives service;
- the place of owner's custody or the sequence of places of custody from origin to transfer;
- the method of transfer of ownership or custody to the archives (e.g. deposit, bequest, rescue) (unless for specific reasons this is given in the accession record);
- in cases of purchase, the price, and source of funding (unless this is given in the accession record);
- the date of transfer to the archives. If it is desired that this should remain confidential, use the accession record instead.
- references to relevant records held in the repository, or to sources of information on the entity.

For examples, see those for the administrative history above (Section 14.3A).

14.3C *Archivist's note*
The purpose of the archivist's note sub-area is to record important facts about the nature of the entity and how it has been treated by the repository.

There are three data elements which note, respectively, the relationships between parts of the entity, how appraisal decisions have been approached and carried out, and how the parts of the entity have been arranged within the repository.

14.3C1 Relational complexity and status
If the archive is related by provenance, hierarchy or function, to a larger unit or to other materials or is part of or an addition to an existing archival entity at a higher level, give the identity statement for that entity. In addition indicate the relationship of the material to the other entity using such phrases as 'forms part of . . .', 'in . . .', 'addition to . . .', and other introductory wording as appropriate.

If the archive is related to other entities for which there are descriptions at a lower level, give a brief explanation of the structure of the group, including the identity statements of entities referred to. Phrases such as 'The group [subgroup, etc.] is divided into classes [subgroups, pieces, etc.] as follows . . .' can be used.

Example:

The records have been arranged in the following categories:

1. Deeds of settlement, Acts of Parliament
2. Directors' minutes and other papers
3. General (shareholders') meetings minutes;
   annual reports and accounts.
4. Secretary's papers
5. Accounts
6. Gas and electricity contracts papers:
   Belgium
   France
   Germany
   Netherlands
   Romania
7. Staff records

Example:

The records comprise minute books, ledgers and other volumes from a racked store room; the contents of metal deed boxes holding deeds and agreements and a variety of other documents, many of them doubtless preserved for their historical interest; and files from a filing cabinet of older files. No records later than 1970 were taken, except for examples of publications. A good series of minute books, many deeds and agreements, and a wide range of ledgers and other financial records have survived.

The headquarters of the Association were in London until 1960 and probably much which survives was consciously selected for transfer to Epsom. Several of the bundles bear numbers which related to a modern brief listing, but there is no evidence of original archival arrangement.

[*Source*: Surrey Record Office]

> Example:
>
> Documents of exceptional size pre-1931 and any supporting items post-1931 form a supplementary class of papers.

Materials related in non-structural or organic ways (e.g. by subject matter) should be cross-referred in the related materials sub-area.

14.3C2 Appraisal principle

Explain the principle upon which appraisal decisions have been made. Where different principles have been applied to different subgroups or classes, give sufficient information on the system of arrangement of the entity to allow users to understand its composition and the relevant finding aids. If the appraisal principle adopted might affect the interpretation of the materials (e.g. if there has been sampling), this should be explained here.

Specific actions arising from appraisal are better placed in the appraisal review record (Section 14.8G).

> Example:
>
> Correspondence files are only retained where they deal with matters of policy or the planning of specific projects. They should in all cases be used in association with the committee minutes and papers.

14.3C3 System of arrangement

Give a brief account of the present and former arrangement of the material in so far as this might affect interpretation.

This is the preferred field for this type of information (in preference to the arrangement record (Section 14.8A) or appraisal review record (Section 14.8G) sub-areas) because it forms part of the moral defence of the archive, and is of direct value to users.

If the system of arrangement finally adopted is not described elsewhere (for example in the administrative history sub-area (Section 14.3A) or in the arrangement record sub-area (Section 14.8A)), make a note of it, specifying the principal characteristics of the internal structure and order, and how these have been treated. If there are subgroups in a group, there may be a list of titles or headings of these. Record the levels of arrangement adopted.

Make a note of the presence and nature of any original finding aid.

Explanation of level numbering used may be appropriately entered here.

Administrative information (for use within the repository) about arrangement should be placed in the arrangement record sub-area.

14.4 Content and character area

This area is intended to record all the other information required to establish intellectual control over the materials, i.e. to enable users to identify the materials they need, and to take measures to retrieve the full information held in the original materials. The precise fullness of detail to be entered depends on the policy of the archives service and the objective of the finding aid being constructed. Rules on depth of description in Part I apply (Section 8).

The content and character area has three sub-areas:

abstract;
diplomatic description;
physical description.

14.4A *Abstract*

The purpose of the abstract is to summarize the content or specific informational character of the materials. The amount of detail or the completeness of this record depends on the purpose of the finding aid and the level of description. Prominent abstracts are characteristic of (but not exclusive to) descriptions at class and below.

The abstract is normally a free text entry, without limitation as to length.

A contents analysis may serve to structure the information which would normally occur in the abstract; in this case, appropriate data elements include:

- *date* (single or covering); dates entered here may be full, detailed or complex.
- *site, locality or place* (the specificity of site identification, or the use of uniform names may be determined by general policy in the archives service: e.g. authority list of place names, geographical coordinates);
- *personal or corporate names*;
- *events or activities*;
- *subject keywords* (these may be provided from an authorized vocabulary, or by reference to an authority list of subject titles).

Include also any information additional to that given in the title sub-area. This may include more precise information on the form of the materials, the names of individuals or organizations (which may appear in the title in their simplest form), or dates. If the date of the original event differs from that of the archival materials which deal with it and which is given in the title sub-area, then record the relevant dates. If the dates given in the date element of the title sub-area (Section 14.2B5) are simplified or in some way do not correspond with dates occurring in the body of the materials, the full dates may be given here within the text.

Record any sources or documents which have been used to assemble information in this area.

Example:

Business correspondence of the Corsini Brothers. During the second half of the sixteenth century the brothers Philip and Bartholomew Corsini operated a considerable import and export business out of their house in Gracechurch Street, fully documented in this correspondence. Agents across Europe corresponded with them in the course of their business activities, occasionally including political or family news along with details of local commercial conditions... It should be noted that from 1582 most of the overseas correspondents used New Style dating while the dates of receipt endorsed on the letters were Old Style.

[*Source*: Guildhall Library Manuscripts Department Corporation of London]

Example:

The statements of assets include inventories and valuations of land, works, machinery, buildings and, where relevant, abstract of supply contracts.
  ... summarizes activity at each European station under the headings leases, shares, staff, accidents, credit, compensation, land, repairs etc.

14.4B *Diplomatic description sub-area*
Diplomatic (diplomatics, diplomatique) is the name of the academic study concerned with the interpretation of documents by means of a technical examination of their form.

This sub-area is provided so that there can be a technically accurate record of the diplomatic character of the archive. Care should be taken to distinguish between the diplomatic and physical description sub-areas, though in many cases there may be little or nothing to record under the former, and the physical description will include all the useful information that is available. The physical description sub-area is preferred where there are no technical considerations in connexion with the form of the materials which relate to the study of diplomatic.

A special format is provided in *MAD* for the detailed description of title deeds (Part V).

This sub-area will normally be treated as free text, and may be given at the end of the abstract. In some cases, where a wide variety of diplomatic forms is not encountered, full descriptions may be replaced by codes or brief headings.

Give notes on the diplomatic of the archival entity, or an indication of its form, type or genre. This entry may refer back to the term of form, type or genre element of the title (Section 14.2B3). In this sub-area more detail may be given.

Terms suitable for use in this sub-area are:

at class level: 'in-letters', 'registered filing system', 'title deeds', 'court rolls', etc.
at item level: 'registered file', etc.
at piece level: 'mortgage'; 'letter', etc.

The following additional data elements may be used in the diplomatic description area:

– problem features, such as missing information, difficulty of interpretation etc;
– predominant language of the material (e.g. Latin);
– characteristic script used (e.g. secretary hand);
– special features, (seals, watermarks, etc.);
– secondary characteristics (e.g. that the materials are copies, or drafts; *n.b.* if these materials are microform or photographic copies, indicate this here, unless it is preferred to make this entry under the access, reference and publication area (Section 14.5), which is preferred unless there is diplomatic relevance.

Example:

Later additions are in a seventeenth century hand.

Example:

Printed English translation of orders recovered from ships scuttled at Scapa Flow in 1918, including manuscript notes, apparently by Jellicoe.

[*Source*: British Library Department of Manuscripts]

Example:

Signed: A White ('Quhyte').
Seal and notarial sign.
Marginal note: 'ultimo Maij 1490'.

[*Source*: Scottish Record Office, Crown Copyright]

Example:

Endorsed: " . . .".
    Seal, said to be affixed, now missing.

14.4C *Physical description*
This sub-area provides for information on the physical shape, size, character and condition of the materials. This information relates to that in the location record sub-area (Section 14.7B). Physical description is the preferred sub-area when user information, rather than process control, is the principal objective.

14.4C1 Physical character
Give a description of the overall physical character of the materials.
    Terms such as 'file(s)', 'volume(s)', 'box(es)', 'bundle(s)', 'loose papers', etc. are appropriate.

14.4C2 Quantity, bulk or size
Give the quantity, extent, size or bulk (dimensions, number, amount) e.g. 10 vols, 150 boxes. The measures used should be those standard in the repository, but if there is no local standard, metric linear measure is the preferred option e.g. 30 m [sc. of shelving].
    The physical character and quantity/bulk/size are usually taken

together. They may occupy dedicated fields in the finding aids, and in this case field lengths may be limited. Both these elements may refer back to the title sub-area (Section 14.2B) or to the location record sub-area (Section 14.7B).

Example:

1 bundle (33 items)
2 items in envelope

14.4C3   Physical condition
Note the physical condition of the entity. Where this in broad terms affects access, a possible area is the access, publication and reference area (Section 14.5); however access restrictions based purely on considerations of physical condition are often better placed here: for example, where ultraviolet light would be necessary to read the materials.

Example:

At level 2: "Extensive water damage caused by poor storage especially affects classes which were kept at floor level: even numbers below 50";

At level 3: "parchment volumes sewn with leather thongs; many pages affected by creasing";

At level 4: "loose binding repaired by local craftsman binder in about 1870";

At level 5: "bottom right corner torn off, obscuring some lines of text".

Cross-reference to the conservation area (Section 14.9) will normally be useful.

14.5 Access, publication and reference area

The purpose of this area is to supply and draw together several categories of information bearing on the use of the original materials, their production to users individually or collectively, and what those users have done with them.

The area may be regarded as intermediate between the archival description sector and the management information sector, since there are circumstances in which a note of these items of information is required as part of the public finding aids, and there are circumstances in which this data would be needed primarily for the control of the materials within the archives service. However, in general this data is needed to support user access, and is in the public domain.

14.5A *Access record*
14.5A1 Access conditions

This sub-area is the preferred one for general statements on access restrictions affected by physical conditions, except where these are very specific: see physical description sub-area (Section 14.4C). Give information on all restrictions that are in force, including general limitations applicable to all users in connexion with this entity, special procedures for permitted classes of user, or conditions of special acccss. Indicate the extent of the period of closure, and the date at which the materials will become open.

Management data on these points, not intended for the information of users who are members of the public, have their preferred place in the issue for use sub-area (Section 14.8D).

Example:

No access may be given to this item without the written permission of a director of the firm.

Whole class embargoed 100 years, calculated from the last entry in each item.

The following classes of more recent records are open to public inspection by statute or usage: . . .

> Example:
>
> Access may be refused to any item which is in need of repair.

14.5A2 Copying conditions
This element is provided to allow the explanation of non-legal restrictions.

Give information on any administrative restrictions on the reproduction of the materials for users or for publication, and indicate the general policy on reproduction as applied to this archive.

14.5A3 Copyright information
This element is appropriate for restrictions of a legal character.

If the copyright situation in respect of these materials is unknown, no statement is necessary. If the rights were dedicated or reserved under a legal instrument, or as a condition of deposit, include a descriptive note. If it is known that the copyright is held by an individual or by a corporate body, details should be given, together with the expiry date, or contingency upon which an expiry date depends.

Cross-reference to the issue for use record sub-area may be made.

14.5B *Publication record*
Give references to cases where the archive has been published or has been cited in publications by users.

If the archive, or part of it, has been or is to be published (including publication on microform, optical disc or any other medium) give the publication details.

Include journal articles describing portions of the materials, guides describing the archival entity in terms of a particular subject focus, or other published descriptions, indexes and calendars. Give bibliographic descriptions of any published version.

Entries in this area are likely to be citations or bibliographical references, and should therefore be made in accordance with appropriate bibliographical standards.

14.5C *Related materials*
14.5C1 Give references to archival or bibliographic materials (possibly including materials in other repositories) or museum objects, etc., which have a close relationship with the materials being described. Indicate the whereabouts and nature of the related

materials. (See also the archivist's note (Section 14.3C), which is the preferred sub-area for notes on the relationship between components of the archive itself.)

14.5C2 If not given in the publication record (Section 14.5B) (which would be the preferred sub-area), or elsewhere, indicate the existence of copies (microfilm, photocopy, transcript).

14.5C3 Give a reference to any other finding aids the repository may have to the organization and contents of the materials being described, including inventories, lists, calendars, class descriptions, card indexes, institutional guides, etc.

14.5C4 If the list has been deposited with and is available for consultation at any other repository or at the National Register of Archives, note this here.

Examples:

There is correspondence from Vice-Admiral Sir Samuel Hood (1762–1814) in the Keats Papers (KEA/10), the McKinley Papers (MCK/11), the Duckworth Papers (DUC/14) and in the museum's collections of single orders and memoranda (HSR/6/11) and letters (AGC/6/17 and 22).

Source: Manuscripts Department, National Maritime Museum

The Zurich catalogue describes further letters addressed to merchants in Italy, with some addressed to a merchant in Antwerp; microfilm copies of some of these are at Mss 21,323–21,326.

Source: Guildhall Library, Department of Manuscripts, Corporation of London

14.5D *Exhibition record*
The purpose of the exhibition record sub-area is to provide an opportunity for a reference to be made to the publication of an archival document by means of exhibition exposure, including formal publication of text or commentary in an exhibition catalogue. Such information is clearly of value to users, and is in the public domain.

Where the record of the exhibition of an archival item is required chiefly as an administrative control the preferred sub-area would be the loan record sub-area (Section 14.8F). This is especially so if there is need for confidentiality, and no need for public user information.

14.5D1 Circumstances
Give details of the circumstances in which the materials were exhibited, including place and date, and a citation for any publications (such as an exhibition catalogue) which referred to them.

The preferred sub-area for administrative information about the loan and return of the materials is the loan record (Section 14.8F).

14.5D2 Physical condition
Give details of any physical changes which occurred to the materials while on exhibit (if this is not dealt with in the conservation area (Section 14.9), which would be the preferred area unless this information was of direct interest to users).

14.6 THE MANAGEMENT INFORMATION SECTOR

The purpose of this sector is to record information needed for controlling the processes carried on within the repository. This includes both information which should be held in a permanent record, and also more ephemeral data. Although in some circumstances users may need some of the information recorded here, it is not regarded as being within the public domain. In general, the archival description sector (Section 14.1) would be preferred for any information of direct value to users, even though it might relate to processes within the repository.

As in the archival description sector, only areas, sub-areas and data elements which are immediately relevant need be used, all others being omitted.

It is not possible to link the level of description closely to the use of management information areas, sub-areas or data elements. There is in principle an assumption that data elements which give very specific information about small quantities of material may be regarded as being most natural to descriptions at item or piece level; but against this, there are certainly situations in which procedural information is needed in group, subgroup or class descriptions. The general rule that any data element may be used at any level of description therefore continues to apply in this sector.

The management information sector has three areas:

(1) The administrative control information area forms the accession record and explains where the material is kept;

(2) the process control area allows the repository to track the archive through the various stages of processing;

(3) the conservation area allows the repository to record conservation needs and track the material through conservation processes.

14.7 Administrative control information area
14.7A *Accession record*
This sub-area deals with information which may as an alternative be wholly or partly recorded in the custodial history sub-area (14.3B).

The accession record is intended to provide information which is both for immediate administrative use and for permanent record. In general, repositories will wish always to maintain an accession register or record, and this sub-area may be used for it, irrespective of whether the custodial history contains accession information. This remains the preferred sub-area where internal control is the main objective, or where there is need for confidentiality.

14.7A1 Allocate or record an accession number, code or reference, which may refer to an accessions register.

The permanent reference code (Section 9.10) of an archival entity, where this is different from the accession number, should be cross-referred to it.

14.7A2 Give the date(s) of accession, or the date on which the materials came into custody. A reference to the location of the accession may be given here, or in the location record sub-area (Section 14.7B) (which is preferred).

14.7A3 Describe the method of acquisition, or terms and conditions (e.g. purchase, gift, loan, deposit, transfer).

14.7A4 Record the immediate provenance or source of the accession, with enough detail to allow cross-reference to the administrative and custodial history.

14.7A5 If there is an agreement with the owner, depositor or originating body, which involves future action, record this here. Such agreements may provide for future contact, the financing or provision of services, etc. If there is no agreement, but it is perceived that there is a need for future contact with the originating body, then describe this situation. The date and nature of any future contact should be given.

14.7A6 If future accruals (Section 9.3) are to be expected, an estimate of their bulk and character and expected date may be given here. Alternatively, these details may appear in the location record (Section 14.7B), especially if space in the repository is to be earmarked. The accession record is the preferred sub-area if future action is to be administered on the basis of this data.

14.7A7   Give details of any source of funding received to encourage or support the accession.

14.7B   *Location record*
14.7B1   Give the place of storage of the materials. In the case of large entities, this may be a complex record.

14.7B2   Give the size, bulk, quantity, volume or extent of the materials, and/or the length of shelving occupied by them. The measures used should be those standard in the repository, but if there is no local standard, metric linear measure of shelving is the preferred option. There may be a cross-reference to the physical description (Section 14.4C). The location record is the preferred sub-area for storage information needed primarily for repository management.

14.7B3   The expected or past rate of accrual may be given here if it does not appear in the accession record sub-area (Section 14.7A). The location record is the preferred sub-area for this, where the information is intended primarily for repository management.

14.8   Process control area

The data elements in this area are intended to provide a record of the completion of the main processing stages which are carried on in the repository. The main aim is repository control, making sure that the various processes are carried out on time, etc.; but generally there may also be a need to record what has been done, as part of the permanent record.

14.8A   *Arrangement record*

This sub-area covers ground which may be dealt with in the archivist's note sub-area (Section 14.3C). This is the preferred sub-area where internal repository management is the main objective, and there is no desire to inform users in general.

14.8A1   Give a brief account of the sorting method adopted for the physical arrangement of the materials, unless this appears in the administrative and custodial history (Section 14.3) or in the content and character areas (Section 14.4). Record the identity of the archivist who was responsible. Note any special problems or features.

14.8A2   Record details of any special funding received or allocated for the processing of this archive.

14.8A3   Give the date(s) of completion of arrangement of the materials.

14.8B   *Description record*

This sub-area records progress made towards the completion of the description process.

14.8B1   Give details of the plan adopted in embarking on the description of the archive. Give the identity of the archivist responsible. This information may as an alternative appear in the content and character area (Section 14.4).

14.8B2   Record any funding received for the completion of this work.

14.8B3   Give the date of completion of the work. Distribution of the descriptions can be added. Record despatch of a copy of the description to the National Register of Archives, if this was not done in the related materials sub-area (Section 14.5C).

14.8C *Indexing record*
If local custom is to treat indexing as a separate process, the work done on this may be recorded here.

Give the name of the person responsible.

Note the system used, or an indication of indexing rules, authority lists or other vocabulary controls.

Give details of any relevant funding received for this operation.

Record the date(s) of completion.

14.8D *Issue for use record*
Information in this area is often most appropriate at item level.

14.8D1 If this information does not appear in the access, publication and reference area (Section 14.5), give details of the access status of this material, and the policy covering its issue to users. This may be useful in cases where the access, publication and reference area refers mainly to the higher levels of arrangement, or to large entities. In this case, the record of issue for use may be used to control individual classes or items for which there is special access provision.

14.8D2 Give the user's identity, and note the fact if there is any special provision covering this transaction.

14.8D3 Give the issue time and date, following local repository practice. If production of the material is outside the main repository, it will be necessary to include the due date for its return.

14.8D4 A record of the number of times an archival or record entity has been consulted may be needed in order to assist appraisal, or to help in managing the repository and its resources.

14.8E *Enquiry record*
This sub-area allows entries which record where there has been reference to the entity in answer to enquires from users.

14.8E1 Give the identity of the enquirer.

14.8E2 Record the subject or purpose of the enquiry.

14.8E3   Give the date at which the reference was made.

14.8F   *Loan record*
This sub-area allows for a record where materials have been loaned for exhibitions or reference in another repository. Some of this information may have been recorded in the access, publication and reference area (Section 14.5). The purpose of the loan record sub-area is to control the administration of the loan. Data held here is not intended for the information of public users.

14.8F1   Give the identity of the person or organization to which the material has been loaned.

14.8F2   Give the date of despatch or issue of the materials.

14.8 F3   Give the date of return, or the date on which return is due or expected.

14.8F4   If relevant, insurance or security details information may be added.

14.8G   *Appraisal review record*
This sub-area is intended for recording the operations, past or future, involved in the appraisal of the archival entity. Section 14.3E is more appropriate for recording the appraisal principle, or general policy involved.

14.8G1   Give the appraisal procedure or house rules which have been used in the case of these materials.

14.8G2   Record the action which has been taken or recommended.

14.8G3   Give the action date, i.e. the date on which future action is to be taken in order to implement the appraisal decision.

14.8G4   Give the identity of the person responsible for the apprai-sal decision.

14.9 The conservation area

The purpose of the conservation area is to provide for a permanent record of the conservation (either environmental or remedial) of archival entities, and to contain information which will help control the conservation processes within the repository.

The conservation area may, like the other areas, be used at any level of description. Its mode of operation will therefore be different when working at different levels. Data which relates to groups, for example (especially when the group in question is large) can only deal in very broad terms with the conservation of the group, and will probably be confined to information in support of environmental or preventative conservation.

Example:

Parts of this group have been exposed to damp over long periods and are fragile.

When the data relates to items or pieces, it is likely to be specific and to deal with repair; it can, indeed, be used to monitor the repair process.

Example:

Rebound 10/1985, as two volumes.

14.9A *Administration*

This sub-area is intended to contain data relating to the management aspects of conservation, in relation to the archival entity being described.

14.9A1 Indicate the general situation of the entity in relation to its physical character; this may include information on the storage conditions under which the entity is or has been kept. Cross-refer to the physical description sub-area (Section 14.4C), and, if necessary, to the administrative records of the repository.

14.9B *Conservation record*

The sub-area is intended to contain information which will allow for the monitoring of conservation processes and repair.

14.9B1   Record the previous conservation history of the entity; however, if public information is intended, these details would be better placed in the physical description sub-area (Section 14.4C).

14.9B2   Indicate details of any repair work required, immediately or in the future.

14.9B3   Indicate the level of priority which is to be given to the work.

14.9B4   Record the name of the conservator responsible.

14.9B5   When repair is done, record the dates on which repair work started and the date on which the materials subjected to repair were returned to their storage location.

14.9B6   Include a description of the repair carried out.

14.9B7   Add any recommendations for future conservation. These may refer to special storage conditions, further repair work, periodic examination, etc.

14.9B8   This sub-area may also be used to record the type and quantity of new materials used in the work of repair, so as to provide control over stocks.

14.9B9   Record any relevant funding received in respect of the conservation or repair of this archive.

PART III
RECOMMENDED DESCRIPTION
FORMATS

15

Recommended description formats

15.1   Archival descriptions are composed by selecting relevant data elements from the table of data elements (Part II) and arranging them in accordance with the models given in this section.

Each archive is unique, and presents special features of its own. It is therefore quite usual for archivists to decide that the listing models cannot be used without some modification to suit the job in hand. *MAD* standards have been devised with this qualification in mind. It is hoped and expected that it will be possible to apply the principles and general rules laid down in *MAD* while at the same time successfully applying local and case-specific modifications to the actual layout of data on the page.

15.2   This part sets out models for description at the principal different levels. Models are therefore provided for

– management group headings	(level 1)
– group and subgroup descriptions	(level 2)
– class descriptions	(level 3)
– item and piece descriptions	(levels 4,5)

Finding aids are composed by putting together archival descriptions covering different levels in different ways. The second part of this section (15.14) illustrates models for the combination of descriptions.

15.3   It is recommended that archivists undertaking description should use the areas and/or sub-areas as wholes, wherever this is suitable (Section 13.6). Individual data elements may be selected without regard to their context in areas or sub-areas, if this suits the work; but it is expected that normally this approach will only be suitable where a computer system incorporating the table of data elements is used.

If data capture forms are to be used, it is recommended that areas and sub-areas should be given distinct boxes or locations on the form, with data elements within them being indicated without emphasis.

15.4 In the following section, the standards for some applications of important general rules are repeated in summary form.

15.5 Macro and micro descriptions

15.5A The need for distinct macro and micro descriptions arises from the multi-level rule, which is explained in Section 5.

15.5B Descriptions at any of the numbered levels may be treated as being macro or micro descriptions, depending on their relationship with other descriptions in the same finding aid. Thus, normally, a group description would be a macro description in relation to its dependent subgroup or class descriptions. However, in other circumstances, a set of group descriptions may be micro in relation to management group headings (e.g. in a repository guide to holdings). The same alternatives apply at all levels.

15.5C Macro descriptions give general and contextual information about sets of archives which belong in related groupings. Such macro descriptions are said to govern the sets of micro descriptions which deal with the components of the entity. This governing function should be demonstrated in the way in which the two kinds of description are set out. Generally, the macro description should precede the related micro descriptions. It can appear separately as a title page or title page section, or it can appear as a headnote (Section 6). Headnotes are laid out in a way which shows that they govern the descriptions that come below them.

15.6 Paragraph or list mode

The difference between paragraph and list mode descriptions is explained in Section 7. Generally, archivists may choose between variations of one of these modes, following the needs of the entity being described, and the local house rules.

15.7 Summary of models

1. Models for description at specific levels
1.	Management group headings	(level 1)
2.	Group descriptions	(level 2)
3.	Subgroup descriptions	(level 2.nn)
4.	Class descriptions	(level 3)
5.	Item descriptions	(level 4)
6.	Piece descriptions	(level 5)

2. Models for the combination of descriptions
1.	Group and subgroup	(levels 2,2nn.)
2.	Group and class	(levels 2,3)
3.	Group and item	(levels 2,4)
4.	Class and item	(levels 3,4)
5.	Item and piece	(levels 4,5)
6.	Three-level descriptions	

15.8   Management group headings (Level 1)

15.8A   (For an explanation of the term 'management group', see Section 4.6B.) Management groups do not have descriptions in the strict sense, because they are not themselves archival entities. Because of this, the term 'heading' is used in relation to them. In practice, finding aid systems do often require descriptive information to be given at management group level (level 1), in order to explain the structure of the system, or to give information on background, context and provenance.

15.8B   Although in principle any area, sub-area or data element may be chosen for inclusion in a level 1 heading, the most characteristic area is the administrative and custodial history (Section 14.3). The heading therefore consists most typically of the following:

Repository name ⎱	
Management group title ⎰	Dedicated fields
Administrative and custodial history area.	Free text

Example:

GLOUCESTERSHIRE RECORD OFFICE
SMALL BOROUGHS AND TOWN TRUSTS

Many small towns and large villages had anciently acquired some of the attributes of borough status but were not accepted as boroughs under the Municipal Corporations Act 1835. Other settlements had bodies of feoffees who acted for the freeholders as owners of common property, as at Upton St Leonards, where the freeholders had purchased the manor in the 16th century.

   The records usually include minutes, accounts and title deeds, and often papers concerning schools and charities.

[*Source:* Gloucestershire Record Office]

15.8C   Where level 1 headings are used, they should if possible contain all the information common to the groups which are contained within them. The group descriptions which follow the heading may then avoid repeating the data given in the heading.

Figure III 15.8 Format for a group description

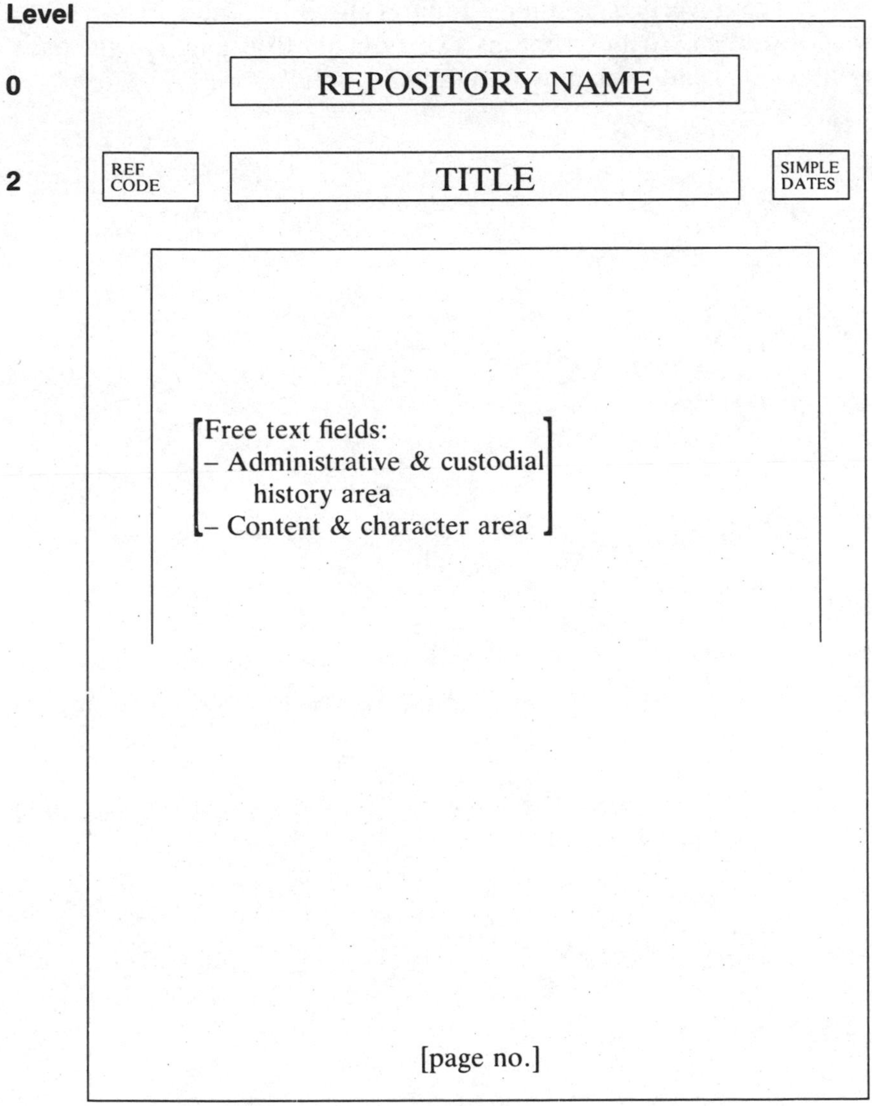
Level
0
2
REPOSITORY NAME
REF CODE
TITLE
SIMPLE DATES
Free text fields:
– Administrative & custodial history area
– Content & character area
[page no.]

15.8D Although the term 'heading' is used for these descriptions, the relationship between them and the sets of (group) descriptions which are governed by them, follows the same rules as for other macro and micro descriptions (Section 5): title pages, title page sections or headnotes may be used (Section 7).

15.9 Group descriptions (Level 2)
15.9A *General shape*

15.9A1 Group descriptions consist essentially of free text, frequently but not always lengthy. In addition to the free text, a small number of dedicated fields may be provided at the top of the (first) page, to contain the name of the repository, and one or more of the elements of the identity statement (reference code, title) (Section 14.2). To these, the level number may be added, for internal use in the repository.

15.9A2 The information given in the dedicated fields may if desired be placed on a title page (Section 6), together with repository information. In this case local practice should be followed as to layout and the inclusion of additional information such as the date of the completion of the description, its author, access information, etc.

15.9A3 In accordance with the general style of *MAD* standards, where there is no separate title page, reference codes should normally appear at the beginning of the description, in the left margin; simple span dates (if used) should either follow the name element after a comma, or should appear in a column on the right margin. If level numbers are used, for internal purposes, they may appear in either margin. It is a recommended practice that these level numbers should be distinguished from references available to users, by using colour codes, distinctive type or bracketing.

15.9A4 There may be further dedicated fields if desired, at the head or foot of the free text section. Fields for quantity, size, bulk and for form, type, genre are particularly suitable.

15.9A5 Within the free text, further structures may be introduced. New paragraphs or headed sections should be used for each area or sub-area. Where the contents of an area are lengthy (as would often be the case in the administrative history) (Section 14.3A), it may be convenient to break the text up into chapters or further headed sections.

15.9A6 Chapter or section headings should be underlined, set in capitals or bold characters, in accordance with local practice, and following a hierarchical ranking. Where chapters or a sequence of

115

headed sections are used, the free text field may be preceded by a contents list.

15.9A7 It is clear from the above, that group descriptions are normally in paragraph mode (Section 7). List mode entries are also possible, where the group descriptions form a set of tabulated headings following a headnote. In this case the central or main text column will contain the title, perhaps followed by a brief entry for the administrative and custodial history (Section 14.3) or content and character areas (Section 14.4).

15.9B *Data elements*

15.9B1 For the structure of data elements, and information on their combination in areas and sub-areas, see Part II. Any of the areas, sub-areas or data elements may be selected for use, but apart from an element of the identity statement (Section 14.2), none are compulsory.

15.9B2 A typical group description uses the data elements which belong to these areas, in the following order. (An index or other retrieval aid is commonly added.)

Identity statement (Section 14.2);
Administrative and custodial history (Section 14.3);
Content and character area (Section 14.4);
[Index].

15.9B3 The identity statement commonly consists of reference code and title. The title sub-area contains three data elements, any or all of which may be used; the data elements comprise a term for form, type or genre; a name element; span dates.
For rules on the choice of titles, see Section 14.2B.

15.9B4 The recommended style is for the name element in the title to be centred, with the reference code at the left margin in a column reserved for reference codes; the name element may be followed by the simple span dates after a comma, or these may be placed in a dates column at the right margin, according to house style. Layouts such as these facilitate scanning. Local house styles should be followed where the standard is not suitable.

116

Example:

		(Level)
dv89	*Borough of Borchester, 1447–1835*	(2)
or		
dv89	Archives of Borchester Town Council	1447–1835

15.9B5 The level number (Section 14.2C) may be used for convenience in-house or for the interchange of descriptions; if given, it should appear in the left or right margin, level with or near to the first line of text, and distinguished from reference code by colour, type or bracketing.

15.9B6 The administrative and custodial history and content and character areas.

Both the administrative and custodial history (Section 14.3) and the content and character areas (Section 14.4) (particularly the abstract sub-area (Section 14.4A) within the latter) relating to a group will normally be free text narrative. It is a useful practice to break up long sections of text by subheadings. Cross-references may be written into dedicated fields, placed in the margins or below the paragraph to which they refer, or in footnotes at the bottom of the page.

Where groups or subgroups exhibit recurrent characteristics or constantly repeated data, they should be presented in a standard order which allows as much as possible of the repeated information to be given in a headnote. Side headings may be used to signal the start of blocks of specific information.

15.9C *Retrieval aids*
15.9C1 Group descriptions (like all free text entries) should normally be indexed.

15.9C2 In accordance with *MAD* recommendations on depth of description (the rule on information retrieval (Section 8.4B)), free text entries should be composed with a view to the inclusion of all keywords likely to be needed for a search. If a controlled or structured index vocabulary is being used, some keywords may have to be rewritten as the appropriate preferred term, or cross-references may be necessary. Keywords may be written into dedicated fields to improve their function as access points. Data elements are available to provide for this usage.

15.9C3 Page formats may be established in accordance with existing house styles and *MAD* recommendations. Dedicated fields where used as distinct entities to contain specific data elements may be given preformatted positions on the page. Each page after the first should contain the group reference code and the page number in addition to the free text entry.

15.9C4 It is good practice to give the name of the archivist responsible for the description, with the date of its completion, at the end of the free text. If there is a compuscript, the file name should be recorded with these data elements.

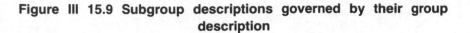

Figure III 15.9 Subgroup descriptions governed by their group description

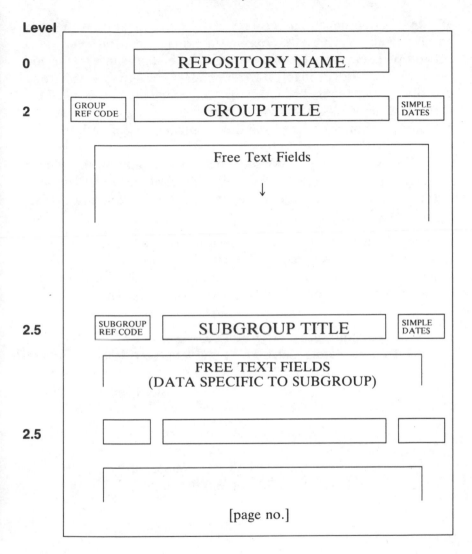

15.10 Subgroup descriptions (Levels 2.nn)
15.10A *General shape*

15.10A1 Subgroups must retain a close connexion with their parent group. (If the description of what has been seen as a subgroup appears capable of standing independently in a finding aid system, it should probably be redefined as a group.) Subgroup descriptions are then framed with this connexion in mind. In a context such as this, the group description acts as headnote and contains all common, background or contextual information.

Each subgroup may in consequence consist only of an identity statement (Section 14.2), but may additionally have an administrative and custodial history (Section 14.3) or content and character area (Section 14.4) of its own.

Subgroup descriptions may be used as headnotes (Section 6) to micro descriptions (Section 5) at class level or below. In this case they take the form of group descriptions, and may repeat or re-use background, contextual or provenance information from the governing group description.

In other circumstances, subgroup descriptions may be treated as distinct and separate entries. Where subgroup descriptions are separated from their covering group descriptions, the text should contain enough common information from the group description, to allow the subgroup description to be intelligible by itself.

Subgroup descriptions are like group descriptions in their general layout. They should contain the elements of the identity statement in dedicated fields, and all other material (where there is any) in a free text entry without length restriction.

15.10A2 The identity of a subgroup may be established by a reference code and one or more elements of the title.

It is recommended that subgroup reference codes, where they are used, should contain an element to indicate the relationship to the parent group. This practice may be omitted if the result would be unduly complex.

For rules on the choice of titles, see Section 14.2B4. Subgroups are normally named from the functional divisions of the group which they represent.

15.10A3 In paragraph mode descriptions (Section 7), subgroups are best treated as free text narrative paragraphs appended to the group description and following their own identity statement.

15.10A4 In list mode descriptions, or where the structure of the group is particularly complex, it may be useful to list subgroup titles as a list of contents immediately after the group description.

15.10B *Data elements*
A minimum content for subgroup descriptions contains data elements from the following areas:

> [Note: in this context, the term 'minimum' does not imply obligation. No area or data element is obligatory in any description except an element of the identity statement.]
> Identity statement (Section 14.2);
> Administrative and custodial history (Section 14.3);
> Content and character area (Section 14.4);
> [Index]

Since subgroup descriptions are normally micro descriptions governed by a group, all common, background or contextual information will appear in the latter. Where subgroup descriptions are used as headnotes to class descriptions or below, such information may be repeated if necessary.

15.10C *Retrieval aids*
An index is commonly added. In normal circumstances the index would relate to the whole group. For examples see Part IV.

Figure III 15.10 Class descriptions, paragraph mode

Level

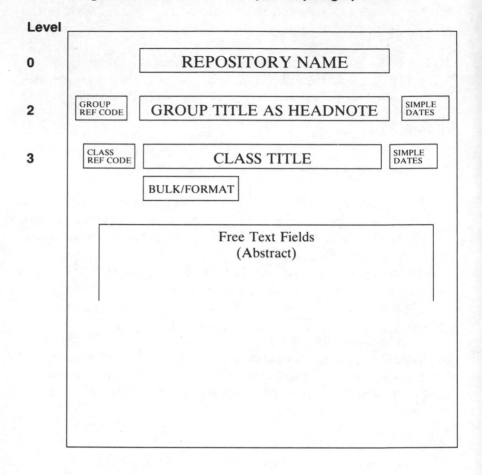

15.11   Class descriptions (Level 3)
15.11A   *General shape*

15.11A1   Class descriptions contain both dedicated and free text fields. At the beginning, dedicated field(s) should contain elements of the identity statement. The main free text field contains the administrative and custodial history area (if relevant) and the content and character area. Other dedicated fields may come before or after the free text field, containing form/genre and bulk/size information. This model constitutes a paragraph mode finding aid, which is therefore regarded as the norm at this level.

15.11A2   List mode is available as an alternative. In this case the title information should appear on the first line. The reference code should occupy the left margin; the simple date or simple span dates should occupy the right margin. The other elements appear in the central (textual) column: it is recommended that the wording here should be underlined or presented in bold type, in order to mark out the title from any other text. This recommendation may be disregarded where a confused page would result. Textual fields containing administrative and custodial history and/or content and character areas appears below the title elements in the central column.

15.11A3   Class descriptions in either mode may serve as headnotes. Layout should follow the rules for composite finding aids: see Section 15.14F.

15.11A4   Class descriptions may also be micro descriptions following a group or subgroup description. Rules for these are in Section 15.14C. In these circumstances *MAD* recommends that the name section of the identity statement may be underlined, or italicized, in order to distinguish the beginning of a new class in the list.

15.11A5   Paragraph and list modes are equally common at this level. Further rules and recommendations are given in the section on composite finding aids (15.14).

15.11B   *Data elements*
15.11B1   A minimum content for class descriptions contains data elements from the following areas and sub-areas:

[Note: in this context, the term 'minimum' does not imply obligation. No area or data element is obligatory in any description except an element of the identity statement.]
Identity statement (Section 14.2);
Content and character area (Section 14.4);
Physical description sub-area (Section 14.4C);
Access condition (Section 14.5A);
[Index]

15.11B2 The identity of a class may be established by a reference code and/or by one or more of the elements of a title.

A class reference code generally appears as a sub-reference of the appropriate group code. There may be intervening subgroup codes, if this addition does not make the reference too complex.

The reference code occupies a dedicated position on the first and every subsequent page, preferably at the head of the left margin. A class reference code generally appears as a subreference of the appropriate group code. There may be intervening subgroup codes, if this addition does not make the reference code too complex (Section 9.10).

For class reference codes used in headnotes, see Section 15.14F.

The title of a class should be given as described in the rules for data elements (Section 14.2B).

The level number, for use in-house, should (where used) be given in one of the margins, level with the reference code or with the first line of text, but distinguished from reference codes by colour code, distinctive type or bracketing.

If there is to be an administrative and custodial history area, it should appear before the content and character area.

15.11B3 The content and character area of a class may contain any or all of the data elements for this area, which is the one most characteristic of class descriptions. Elements which are common to all or many classes in a group are best included in the macro description covering them, or otherwise in a headnote.

15.11B4 Descriptions at class level are the main instruments for both administrative and intellectual control of archives. Group/subgroup descriptions do not usually give direct retrieval information about specific physical entities of archive material. Class descriptions are usually the highest level at which this is done, though to retrieve particular items, a further, more detailed, level of description is usually needed.

For the same reason, it is normal (but not obligatory) for the physical description area to be present. Physical descriptions should cover the whole class. Physical descriptions which refer only to particular items or pieces should appear at that level.

In accordance with the rules on depth of description (Section 8), textual fields in class descriptions should, if possible, contain all keywords required for searches or for index construction. The abstract sub-area may be structured to promote this, using the appropriate data elements, and making allowance for permitted vocabularies.

Figure III 15.11 Class descriptions, list mode

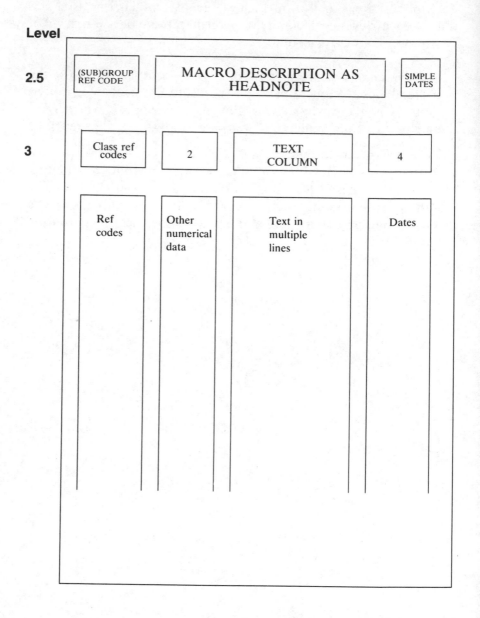

15.12   Item descriptions (Level 4)
15.12A   *General shape*
The minimum content of an item description contains one or more elements from the following areas:

> [Note: in this context, the term 'minimum' does not imply obligation. No area or data element is obligatory in any description except an element of the identity statement.]

Identity statement (Section 14.2);

Content and character area (Section 14.4).

> [Index]

In the identity statement, an item reference code usually refers back to the group/subgroup and class. It would be normal for each item to have a unique subnumber within the class, since this is usually the call number by which the item is retrieved and produced for readers.

The name element of an item title is derived as described in the rules for data elements (Section 14.2B4). In the absence of a name element, it is quite usual for items not to have titles but instead to have a brief abstract or summary of content.

15.12B   *List mode descriptions*
15.12B1   Macro descriptions governing item lists are normally provided as headnotes, though title page sections are possible, especially where there is extensive text.

15.12B2   List mode item descriptions are typically set out in tabulated columns. A full reference code should appear on each page, preferably at the top left margin. Reference code subnumbers which relate to items should appear against each entry, in the left-hand column. If the full reference code is abbreviated, the item subnumber should appear in the character space directly below the subnumber in the main code (see examples in Part IV); however, where users might find this difficult to interpret, it may be best to repeat the full reference code against each item.

15.12B3   Simple span dates, or simple year dates should normally appear in a dedicated column at the right of the page. Complex dates are better treated as text, and written into the main text column. Where the governing macro description contains intelligible

Figure III 15.12 Item descriptions, paragraph mode

Level

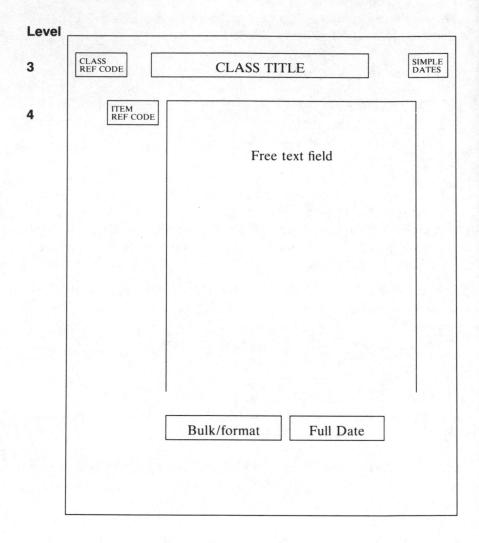

3

CLASS
REF CODE

CLASS TITLE

SIMPLE
DATES

4

ITEM
REF CODE

Free text field

Bulk/format

Full Date

Figure III 15.12B Item descriptions, list mode

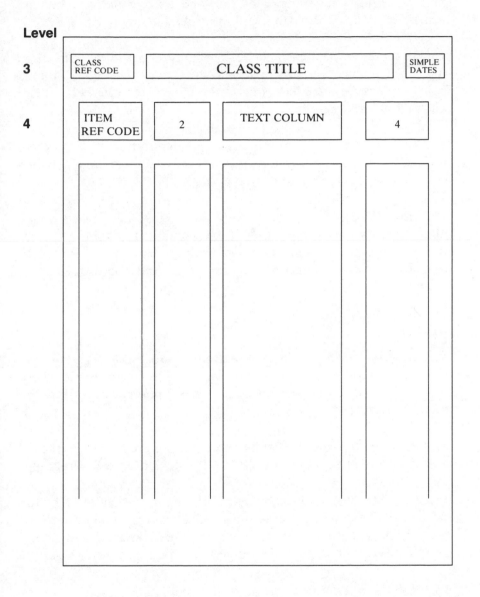

and relevant span dates above the item description, it may be preferable to write item dates into the text of the content and character area, in order to avoid multiple date columns.

15.12B4   Other columns may be chosen as required, but may often include columns for size/bulk and form/type/genre. Additional columns may be included as needed, subject to space being available across the page.

15.12B5   If the diplomatic or physical description sub-areas are used, their entries should appear under the main text column which contains the contents and character area.

15.12B6   Where page layout permits, tabulated item lists which appear below headnotes should be contained within narrower margins, both left and right, than the headnote, in order to emphasize the relationship between macro and micro description fields.

15.12C   *Paragraph mode descriptions*
15.12C1   Where item descriptions contain textual fields longer than six lines, or when the item descriptions are used singly, or are grouped separately from the main finding aids (for example where they are published as a distinct set of descriptions), the paragraph mode is preferred.

15.12C2   In the identity statement, the reference code should appear in the left margin, or as the first element in the paragraph.

15.12C3   All other areas may follow in the order established by the table of data elements. The administrative and custodial history and the content and character areas are normally free text, and should be in consecutive sentences arranged in paragraphs as necessary.

15.12C4   Elements subsequent to the diplomatic description sub-area may be entered in limited-length fields if this is desirable. Such fields may constitute short paragraphs.

15.12C5   Related sets of item descriptions will normally be indexed.
   For examples, see Part IV.

15.12D For both modes, successive pages of a list should preferably include the repository title, and the group/subgroup/class
reference code at the top, and a page number at the bottom.

Where an item list contains a reference to special format, see
Part V.

15.12D1 Item descriptions within a class and containing textual
entries should generally be indexed. Free text fields, such as item
titles, should contain all the keywords necessary for searches or
index construction. Alternatively, keywords may be provided in a
separate field or column.

15.13 Piece descriptions (Level 5)

15.13A The rules for piece descriptions follow those for items.

15.13B A list mode is usual where piece descriptions follow a headnote. Governing macro descriptions in the headnote are normally of the related item, but there may also be cases where linked item and piece descriptions appear together. For composite finding aids see Section 15.14G.

15.13C A paragraph mode is most appropriate where there will be more than one to six lines of text, or where the distant user is principally in mind. Governing macro descriptions may be as above in Section 15.12.

15.14 Composite descriptions
15.14A *Combining description at different levels*

15.14A1 Sets of descriptions of archives are combined into finding aids. Descriptions at two or more levels may be combined into a single finding aid. There are normally at least two levels of description in any finding aid. Three or more levels of description may commonly be found within a finding aid, and there is no restriction on the number of levels which may be so combined, subject to the following rule.

15.14A2 Where two levels of description are provided, covering the same set of related original materials, the higher level should be treated as a macro description governing the lower as micro, in accordance with the multi-level rule (Section 5). This rule also applies where the lower level description itself comprises two levels. Macro descriptions within composite finding aids are displayed as headnotes within the text. Wherever possible, such headnotes should be given wider margins, left and right, than the micro descriptions they govern, in order that the progression of levels, and the hierarchical relationships these express, should be demonstrated.

15.14B *Finding aids containing group and subgroup descriptions (level 2)*
15.14B1 The simplest appropriate method of combining these levels should be adopted.

15.14B2 Subgroups are intimately linked to groups (of which they are organic parts) and the group description will normally include an explanation of the subgroup structure. This explanation should be situated in the administrative and custodial history area (where it arises from an analysis of the original system) and/or the content and character area (where it is an aspect of the description of the content and meaning of the archive). It may contain a specific reference to the subgroups, identifying them by their reference codes and one or more elements of their titles.

15.14B3 If subgroup references are not embedded in the text in this way, they may be distinguished by adding a list of subgroup references and titles at the end of the main text of the group description.

15.14B4   Alternatively, subgroup descriptions may appear in full, in structural, logical or alphabetical sequence after the group description.

15.14B5   If there is an overall title page, it may include a list of subgroup titles immediately following the title of the group they belong to.

15.14C   *Group (subgroup) and class descriptions (levels 2,3)*
15.14C1   The simplest appropriate method of linking group, subgroup and class descriptions should be adopted.

15.14C2   A choice may be made between list and paragraph mode. Where the group or subgroup description acts as headnote to the class description, paragraph mode may be appropriate for the macro description, and list mode for the micro description.

15.14D   *Paragraph mode*
15.14D1   Paragraph mode is appropriate where textual fields contain more than one to six lines of text.

15.14D2   The group/subgroup description which covers the class description set may appear as title page section or as headnote. Alternatively a special headnote may be used, which contains a reference to the full group/subgroup description.

15.14D3   Paragraph mode class descriptions are entered in structural, logical or alphabetical sequence without indentation.

15.14D4   The full reference code should appear on each page, preferably in the top left hand corner. Page numbers should be given, preferably at the bottom of the page.

15.14E   *List mode*
15.14E1   List mode finding aids are made up of headnote (or title page) and tabulated columns.

15.14E2   The left-most column on the page should be dedicated to reference codes. The full code should appear at the head of each page. Codes appropriate to each class should appear on the first line of the class description, and may be limited to that part of the code specific to the class. If this is done, the class number should be printed in the character column below the class reference element in the full reference code at the top of the page. However, user convenience may suggest that the full reference code should be given against each class heading.

15.14E3   Write the class title in the main tabulated column, which should be as broad as possible in order to contain free text. The name element of class titles should be underlined, in bold type or italicized, in order to mark the individuality of the class. This rule may be ignored if it would result in an excessively complex page layout. Additional text comprising entries in the administrative and custodial history and/or content and character areas may appear in the central column immediately below the title.

15.14E4   The simple span date element of the title should normally appear in a right-hand tabulated column, in order to assist scanning by users. Simple span dates consist of four figure year numbers, e.g.

1594–1807

(See Section 14.2B5.)

15.14E5   After the last class description, the list should be completed by an end marker. It is recommended that this should take the form of a brief entry identifying the archivist responsible and the date of completion, e.g.

H. Jenkinson
15 May 1986

15.14F   *Class and item descriptions (levels 3, 4)*
15.14F1   List mode

15.14F1a   The normal format for list mode entries is for the class description to appear as headnote above the text of the list. Alternatively the headnote may be specially written, and cross-refer to the relevant class description. Headnotes governing list mode descriptions may themselves be in paragraph mode, but in any case should use wider margins than the descriptions governed by them. It is generally recommended that the name element of class titles used as macro descriptions should be underlined or italicized.

15.14F1b   Item descriptions in list form which are governed by a headnote should be entered immediately below that headnote.

Example:

XC20/5/1–90   *Corn Rolls*   1919
> Gives by parish, names of holdings, occupiers, landowners, statistics of acreages, labour and livestock, notes on soil fertility...
> 1   Maenan
> 2   Llanrhychwyn
> 3   Trefriw, Abbey and Llanrychwyn
> 4   Dolywddelen
> 5   Eidda

Source: Gwynedd Archives Service

15.14F1c If this page layout is considered too restrictive, owing to the need to compress text within narrow margins, the alternative form below may be considered. In this case, the item numbers are indented beneath the text of the headnote.

XC/20/5/1–90   *Corn Rolls*   1919
Gives by parish, names of holdings, occupiers, landowners, statistics of acreages, labour and livestock, notes re soil fertility...
1 Maenan
2 Llanrhychwyn
3 Trefriw, Abbey and Llanrychwyn
4 Dolywddelen
5 Eidda

15.14F1d The important consideration in any format decision is the need to demonstrate visually the dependence of micro descriptions upon their governing macro description.

15.14F1e The reference code at class level should contain the item level subnumbers expressed as a span. Where bulk is not specifically expressed this also gives some indication of the quantities involved. e.g.

XC20/5/1–90

At the left-hand end of the line, the item number element in the reference code should appear in the character column below the item number element in the full reference code.

Example:

TB3/13–15   *Register of admissions*   1816–1859
  13   1816 Oct 4–1835 Dec 9
  14   1835 July 14–1846 Aug 12
  15   1846 Mar 2–1859 Nov 20

15.14F1f   Individual or span dates of items, if they can be expressed simply, may appear in the right-margin date column. If they are complex, or if the right-margin column is crowded, they may be written into the main text column as content/character area data elements.

15.14F1g   If user convenience requires, full reference codes may be given for each item.

Example:

TB3/13–15   *Register of admissions*   1816–1859
TB3/13   1816 Oct 4–1835 Dec 9
TB3/14   1835 July 14–1846 Aug 12
TB3/15   1846 Mar 2–1859 Nov 20

15.14F1h   There should be one or more blank lines between each set of related class and item descriptions. As in Section 15.14F1d, the intention is to emphasize visually the dependence of micro upon their governing macro descriptions. The overall effect of the page should be to demonstrate that the headnote and list entries belong in a single related section, distinct from the rest of the list.

15.14F2   *Paragraph mode*

15.14F2a   The rules applicable to group/subgroup and class descriptions apply, except that where class descriptions appear as headnotes to item descriptions, the latter should be indented from the left margin.

An example is in Part IV.

15.14G *Item and piece descriptions (levels 4, 5)*
15.14G1 The rules for class/item descriptions (Section 15.14F) apply, both in list and paragraph modes.

15.14G2 In some classes, items and pieces must be treated as equivalent. This might be the case, for example, where the class contains a number of items which consist of pieces bound together, but also a number of unbound pieces. Also, data exchange programmes may demand that no distinction be made between items and pieces. In this case, lists may exist in which items and pieces are treated as on the same level (indicated as level 4/5), and governing macro descriptions may be composed from related class descriptions.

15.14H *Three-level finding aids*
15.14H1 Sets of descriptions which include three or more levels are frequently met (see Section 15.14A2). Any combination of the main levels may occur. The principle is that related macro-micro descriptions should be kept together and nested within the main finding aid.

15.14H2 Either list or paragraph mode may be used.

15.14I *List mode*
15.14I1 The rules for class/item finding aids apply, except that a further indentation should if possible be provided at the third level. This can only be done if the paper width allows the layout without waste or crowding.

Examples are in Part IV.

15.14J *Paragraph mode*
15.14J1 The rules for group/class (Section 15.14C) or class/item (Section 15.14F) finding aids apply, except that there should be an indented left margin at each level.

Examples are in Part IV.

Figure III 15.14 Multi-level descriptions, list mode

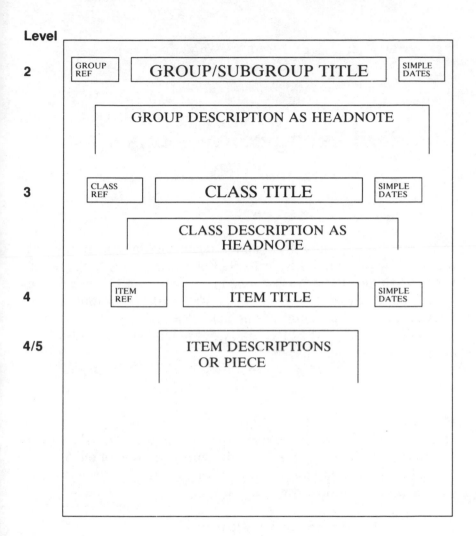

16

Standard listing conventions

16.0 Finding aids should use standard conventions and authorities wherever possible and it is desirable that these conventions should follow existing models in use nationally. There are several such models, and these have been acknowledged at the foot of the relevant tables. Where there is no acknowledgement, the data has been taken from revised PRO practice. Models for the conventions are listed in the bibliography.

16.1 Spelling
16.1A English words should be spelt as in the *Oxford English Dictionary* and its *Supplements*, or the current edition of the *Shorter Oxford English Dictionary*. The following list is of preferred spellings used in record-based work:

    acknowledgement (not acknowledgment)
    appendixes (not appendices)
    chase (not chace)
    dovecote (not dovecot)
    enclosure (not inclosure)
    endorse (not indorse)
    gaol (not jail)
    judgment (not judgement)
    medieval (not mediaeval)
    mottoes (not mottos)
    recognizance (not recognisance)

16.1B In passages quoted from foreign language documents, letters should be given the accents used there. Words of foreign origin which appear with accents in the Oxford dictionaries should also be given them. Where alternative spellings without accents are allowed, these should be preferred.

16.2 Punctuation
16.2A Standard abbreviations, should if possible be drawn from a permitted list. Non-standard abbreviations (e.g. initials of first names) may have full stops e.g.

B. Williams esq

16.2B Entries in free text fields, like other natural-language text, should use normal punctuation, and should have a full stop at the end of the field.

16.2C Within the administrative and custodial history, and the content and character areas, double quotation marks indicate data transcribed from the original. Wording within such quotation marks, including reference codes or titles, should be reproduced exactly as in the original text e.g.

letter headed "3× 2/4 Mr Jone's"

16.2D Information supplied by the editor of a text, or by an archivist compiling a description, as a result of inference or research into other sources, or derived from an investigation of the archival entity being described, should be enclosed in square brackets. A note on the grounds for making the inference may be useful e.g.

[c.1936: endorsed note refers to abdication crisis].

16.3 Capital letters
16.3A Capital letters should be used for proper names, titles of honour when referring to a specific individual, and for acronyms according to the predominant usage of the body e.g.

William Duke of Albany
Unesco, but NATO
Department of Trade and Industry
1st Battalion The Grenadier Guards (where an upper case 't' is consistently used in the title).

16.3B Lower case should be used for titles used in a general or generic sense, and generally where there is room for choice e.g.

the dukes of Albany
municipal corporations and town councils
quarter sessions
census returns

16.3C Upper case characters and underlining may be used to emphasize or pick out significant wording in the body of the text of a description. This practice may be an aid to scanning. (However, where class titles are underlined in a composite list, care should be taken that additional underlining is not confusing.) E.g.

4 acres in the par of WEST KIRBY.

16.4 Numerals
16.4A Generally, all quantities in archival descriptions should be expressed in arabic numerals, and numerals are preferred to written numbers e.g.

4 messuages, 23 vols; *not* four messuages, twenty-three vols.

16.4B Ranges of numbers (e.g. as in reference codes, or in free text) should be expressed in full e.g.

D12/132–139 (not D12/132–9)

16.5 Measurements
16.5A To express physical dimensions, metric measurements are preferred. Measurements referred to in the archive should be retained in their original form.

16.5B Decimals should be preferred to fractions, particularly small or complex fractions e.g.

66.05 (not 66 1/20, unless in direct quotation)

16.6 Dates

16.6A The special rules applying to title dates can be found in the Data Elements summary at Section 14.2B5. . . .

16.6B In archival description generally, broader date ranges are preferable to narrower ones: use the year alone when month and day are not strictly required in the context.

16.6C *Span dates*: Span dates in the text are used if there are no significant chronological gaps in the sequence being described:

> 1643–1687
> 1945 Aug 15–1948 Sept 16
> 1957 Nov 4–1961 Dec 12 and 1971 Mar 2
> 25 Mar–6 Apr 1782
> 4–10 July 1814

16.6D Span dates and single dates entered into the right-hand tabulated column of lists should normally be confined to simple year four-figure numbers. Where fuller or more complex dates are needed, this more detailed date can be entered into a text field such as the Abstract.

16.6E Span dates in right-hand tabulated columns should ignore minor gaps in a chronological sequence. However, significant gaps should be indicated, and the bulk dates separated by semi-colons e.g.

> 1699;1827–1847;1961

16.6F When year, month and day are required, the (abbreviated) month should be written in letters, and placed between the numeral of the day and the numeral for the year. The order year-month-day is preferable to the order day-month-year, but both forms are permissible e.g.

> 1660 May 14
> 31 Jan 1884

16.6G Where an automated system is being used, the year date should always appear first. The International Standard ISO 2014–1976E *Writing of calendar dates in all-numeric form* recommends the use of eight figure dates e.g. 1882.02.07 = 1882 Feb 7), but care should be taken with systems of American origin where the month/day order is reversed (i.e. 1882.02.07 = 1882 July 2).

143

16.6H *Uncertain and inferred dates*: Where no date is available, indicate this by 'undated' or 'no date' (nd); but wherever possible follow this by an approximation in square brackets e.g.

undated	[?1 857]	
	[183–]	decade certain
	[156–?]	decade probable
	[13—]	century certain
	[17—?]	century probable

16.6I Square brackets – [ ] – can also be used to indicate inferred dates. Any or all of the parameters in a date, or parts of them, may be bracketed:

[1842] Jan 2   1842 [Jan] 2
1842 Jan [2]   1842 [Jan 2]
184[2]

16.6J A similar rule operates with questionable inferences where '?' precedes the doubtful element:

[?1842] Jan 2   1842 [?Jan 2]
184[?2]   18[?4]2

16.6K When the date of a document must lie within a specific timespan e.g. a particular reign or a directorship etc., note this. The format '1156 × 1204' can be used to indicate this (e.g. 3 × 15 Ric II).

16.6L 'Temp' (= tempore) should be reserved for dates known only to have been in a particular reign or period e.g.

temp Jas I
temp Duke Humphrey

16.6M 'Circa' should be used (abbreviated to 'c' or 'c.') before a date which, on the balance of probability, is more likely to be correct than the one before or the one after it:

c1636
c1314 May 13
c.3 Ric II

16.6N *Double year-dating*: Where the date before 1752 is between 1 January and 24 March, give the equivalent modern year with the old year date e.g.

> E.g. 1711/12 Feb 2
> 14 Mar 1641/2

[NS = new style, and OS = old style, should be reserved for distinguishing between the Julian and Gregorian calendars e.g. 2 Sept 1752 OS; 14 Sept 1752 NS.]

16.6O For financial or academic years or similar 'overlapping' year date spans, give both calendar years in full, separated by an oblique stroke

> e.g. 1636/1637; 1982/1983

16.6P *Biographical dates*: Dates of an individual's birth and death, when used, are placed in round brackets:

> Smith, John (1924–)
> Smith, John (1837–1896)
> Smith, John (1836 or 1837–1896)
> Smith, John (?1837–1896)
> Smith, John (c 1837–1896)
> Smith, John (b 1837) or (d 1896)
> Smyth, John (fl 1456–1490)
> Smeth, John (bap 1669)

16.6Q *Regnal years*

Wm I (etc)	Phil & Mary
Hen I (etc)	Eliz I (etc)
Stephen	Jas I (etc)
Ric I (etc)	Chas I (etc)
John	Wm & Mary
Edw I (etc)	Anne
Mary	Geo I (etc)
	Vict

> e.g. 1 & 3 Phil & Mary
> 3 Ric III

16.6R *Months*

Jan	July
Feb	Aug
Mar	Sept
Apr	Oct
May	Nov
June	Dec

16.6S *Weekdays*

Mon
Tues
Wed
Thurs
Fri
Sat
Sun

16.6T *Law terms, return days etc.*

Hilary	Hil	
Easter	Easter	
Trinity	Trinity	
Michaelmas	Mich	
octave	oct	e.g. oct Trin 1364
quindene	quin	
morrow	mor	
vacation	vac	

16.6U *Quarter Days:*

English	*Scottish*
Christmas	Candlemas
Lady Day	Whitsun
Midsummer	Lammas
Michaelmas	Martinmas

16.7   Place names

16.7A   *British and local place names*: repositories are recommended to construct and use local authority lists for place names.

16.7B   *Foreign place names*: place names should be cited in commonly accepted forms as given in the current edition of *The Times Atlas of the World*. It is sometimes difficult to decide how foreign place names should be spelt, but a consistent practice should always be followed. Where the form appearing is no longer in current use, the old name should be shown together with the new name in brackets e.g.

Smyrna (Izmir).

Where the change in name has been associated with changes in national boundaries, the new country should also be shown e.g.

Stettin (Szczecin, Poland).

However, a well-established English form should always be preferred to a native one, e.g. Milan, not Milano; The Hague, not Den Haag or 'sGravenhage; Lisbon, not Lisboa.

16.8 Common abbreviations

16.8A Lists of general abbreviations should be followed. Abbreviations which relate particularly to archival description including the following.

16.8B Abbreviations of all kinds should be avoided in free text fields, on title pages or in headnotes. Where a description calls for the use of specialized abbreviations these should be explained in a key provided at the highest level of description, in a headnote, or in a list placed before main passages of text.

16.8C Standard abbreviations are used wherever possible in lists or in dedicated fields.

16.8D The following is a list of recommended common abbreviations specially applicable to non-specialist general archives:

abg	abutting
arr	arranged, arrangement
abp	archbishop
b	born
bap	baptized
bp	bishop
bt	baronet
bd	board
bdl	bundle
betw	between
bldg	building
bro	brother
bur	buried
cent	century
co	company
(C)	copyright
c or c.	circa
corp	corporation
corr	correspondence
cte	committee
cty	county
d	death, died
decd	deceased

deforc	deforciant
dept	department
dist	district
div	division
doc	document
dupl	duplicate(d)
E	east
edn	edition
educ	education
esq	esquire
exor(s)	executor(s)
execx	executrix(es)
f(f)	folio(s)
fl	floruit
gen	general
geneal	genealogical
gent	gentleman
gt	great
husb	husband(man)
inc	includes, including
incorp	incorporated
jun	junior
kt	knight
lre(s)	letter(s)
m	marriage, married
misc	miscellaneous
ms(s)	manuscript(s)
mtg	meeting
N	north
nat	national
nd	no date
nr	near
occ	occupation
p(p)	page(s)
par	parish
pr	printed
pt	part
pub	published

r	recto
reprod	reproduction, reproduced
Rev	reverend if with surname
S	south
sec	secretary
sen	senior
sig	signature
sis	sister
soc	society
suppl	supplement(ed)
ts(s)	typescript(s)
v	verso
var	various, variant
vol(s)	volume(s)
W	west
witn	witness
yeo	yeoman

PART IV
TYPOLOGY OF ARCHIVAL DESCRIPTIONS

Part IV

Typology of archival descriptions

Part IV contains examples of different types of archival description. Each of these has been derived from actual practice in working repositories. The repository which is the origin of the description is acknowledged at the foot of each example, but most descriptions have been edited and in some cases altered (with permission), so as to increase the capacity of the example to illustrate *MAD2* principles and rules.

Figure IV.1: A list of typical management group titles

(a) Local authority record office

Level		
1		Court of Quarter Sessions
	1.5	The court in session
	1.5	Administration
	1.5	Enrolment, registration and deposit
	1.5	Justices of the peace
	1.5	Clerk of the peace
1		Other courts
	1.5	Petty sessions
	1.5	Coroners
	1.5	County courts
1		Statutory authorities
	1.5	Boards of Guardians
	1.5	Turnpike trusts
	1.5	Local boards of health
1		Medical authorities
	1.5	Area health authorities
	1.75	Hospital committees
1		Ecclesiastical
	1.5	Roman Catholic
	1.5	Church of England
1		Families and estates
1		Businesses

(b) Specialist repository.

1		Administration (records generated internally)
1		International
1		Atmospheric sciences
1		Earth sciences
	1.5	Topographical survey
1		Life sciences
	1.5	Biologists' papers
1		Deposited and donated records

[*Source:* British Antarctic Survey Archives]

Figure IV.2: A management group heading

Level

0   NOTTINGHAMSHIRE RECORD OFFICE

1   PU   POOR LAW

Poor Law Unions were set up by the Poor Law Amendment Act 1834. They were dissolved in 1930 under the terms of the Local Government Act 1929 and their poor law functions were transferred to county and county borough councils.
(See CC3/29, CC4/1,17, CC/SS...)

Individual unions:
PUB Basford
PUD Bingham
PUE East Retford
                etc

[*Source*: Nottinghamshire Archives Office]

Figure IV.3: Group descriptions

(a) Institutional (Figure IV.3.1)

DBHB/5   KINGSTON STEAM TRAWLING COMPANY   1891–1973
The company was incorporated in 1891. Hellyer Bros acquired a majority shareholding in 19[?] and the company was absorbed into Associated Fisheries when Hellyer Bros merged with that company in 1961. It ceased trading in 1965 and was dissolved in 1973.
The group includes records of holdings and transfers of shares and proceedings of the board of directors, with some annual reports and accounts.

[*Source*: Hull City Archives]

(b) Personal papers (Figure IV.3.2)

```
360J   MENDELSON                                      1949–1976
       Papers of John Mendelson, MP (1917–1978).
       John Mendelson was born (as Jakob M.) of
       Jewish parents at Plock, Poland. He came to
       England in 1939, after a spell in a refugee
       camp at Zbaszun, and completed his educa-
       tion at the London School of Economics. He
       worked for a time as an extra-mural lecturer
       for Cambridge University prior to his call-up in
       1943. After initial service in the Pioneer Corps,
       he transferred to the Royal Army Education
       Corps in which he was commissioned in 1947.
       Most of his post-war experience was at the
       College of the Rhine Army, Gottingen.
       In 1949 he was appointed as a staff tutor
       in the Department of Extra-Mural Studies,
       Sheffield University, a post he held until
       June 1959 when he won the Penistone bye-
       election in the Labour interest. He held the
       seat until his sudden death in 1978. J. M. was
       on the left wing of the Labour Party and was
       an active member of the Tribune Group. He
       was a member of the Labour Party delega-
       tion to the Council of Europe 1973–77 and to
       the Western European Union 1973–76.
       The group includes papers relating to his
       personal affairs, the conduct of Penistone
       constituency and elections there, and a
       number of photographs of overseas visits
       and lecturing engagements.
       Some parts of the group are subject to
       access restrictions.
```

[*Source*: Sheffield Record Office]

(c) Group descriptions in list mode (Figure IV.3.3)

Level			
1		PRIVATE ARCHIVES	
1.5		<u>FAMILY AND ESTATE ARCHIVES</u>	
2	DAL	Aldersey of Aldersey Mainly title deeds of estates in and around Aldersey and Bunbury.	13–19 cent
2	DAR	Arderne of Alvanley and Harden Title deeds, estate and family papers of the Done, Crewe and Arderne families, estates in and around Utkinton, Delamere Stockport.	13–20 cent
2	DBN	Brooke of Norton Mainly title deeds of estates in Runcorn.	1553–1891

[*Source*: Cheshire Record Office]

Figure IV.4: Subgroup descriptions

(a) Paragraph mode (Figure IV.4.1)

Level		
2	BOARD OF TRADE	
2.5	601.2.16 Fisheries Departments	1867–1903

2.5   601.2.16 Fisheries Departments   1867–1903
Sea fisheries were the responsibility of the Commercial Department until 1867, when they were transferred to the Harbour Department. In 1875 the Board of Trade took over responsibility for shellfish industries and in 1886 that for salmon and freshwater fisheries from the Home Office and in the latter year a Fisheries Department was established to perform these functions. In 1887 it took over from the Marine Department questions relating to fishing vessels and their crews. In 1896 it took over wreck, harbour loans and quarantine duties from the Harbour Department, with which it was united in 1898 to form the Fisheries and Harbour Department. Responsibility for fisheries was transferred to the Board of Agriculture (501) by the Board of Agriculture and Fisheries Act 1903. The Board of Trade's remaining duties relating to fishing vessels, international regulations and general fishery questions passed to the Marine Department in the same year.
Correspondence and papers of the department are in MAF12, MAF41 and MAF71 with a few others in BT13.

[*Source*: Public Record Office, Crown Copyright]

(b) Subgroup descriptions in list mode (Figure IV.4.2)

Level			
2	387	PEA	Papers of Captain George Peacock, 1805–1893.
2.5		P	Papers relating to his career, and biographical notes.
2.5		E	Papers relating to his explorations and surveys.
2.5		I	Papers relating to his inventions and ideas.
2.5		B	Papers relating to Messrs Peacock & Buchan, manufacturers of compositions for ships' bottoms.
2.5		S	Papers relating to the *Swan of the Exe*.
2.5		W	Papers relating to Exmouth Warren.

[*Source*: Liverpool City Archives]

Figure IV.5: Class descriptions

A class description in paragraph mode (Figure IV.5.1)

POWE 14 Electricity Division, correspondence and papers.	1898–1974

      787 files.

Files relating to administration and legislation, electric lighting companies, distribution charges, metering, overhead lines, power stations and generating plant. Some earlier files of the Harbour Department of the Board of Trade and the Electricity Branch of the Ministry of Transport and the Electricity Commission are included in this class. The class also includes the papers of the Committee of Inquiry into the Electricity Supply Industry in England and Wales, 1954–1956.
See also POWE 11–13.
Some items closed for 50 years.

[*Source*: Public Record Office, Crown Copyright]

Class descriptions in list mode (Figure IV.5.2)

Level				
2	D/S	LIVERPOOL SHIPOWNERS ASSOCIATION	1888–1964	
		Founded 1810, incorporated 1888.		
		[Administrative/custodial history cont]		
2.5		*Liverpool Shipowners Freight, Demurrage and Defence Association* c.1845–1917		
2.75		Administration		
3		1–3 *Minute books*	1895–1917	
		3 vols		
3		4–7 *Board agendas register*	1902–1903	
		Some damaged by damp		
2.75		Finance		
3		8–10 *Subscriptions & expenses account books*	1895–1917	

[*Source*: National Museums & Galleries on Merseyside]

Figure IV.6: Item descriptions

Item descriptions in paragraph mode (Figure IV.6.1)

Level **3**	PS2/2 2/1	Minute books	1796–1797
		Minute book of sessions held at Chipping Barnet including Special Licensing Session, 19 Sept 1796, of the Liberty of St Albans for the parishes of Chipping Barnet, East Barnet, Ridge, Northaw and Elstree. The business transacted by the justices is partly administrative, namely appointing parish officials, passing accounts and approving rates, and partly criminal. Cases heard include non-payment of rates, vagrancy, use of false weights, riotous assembly and theft. 1 vol, 24 Feb 1796–10 Aug 1797.	

[*Source*: Hertfordshire Record Office]

Item descriptions in list mode (Figure IV.6.2)

AC6/1/3 **Level**		Pickled herring trade in Germany. Report of a visit to the principal importing centres by the Fishing Officer of Imperial Secretary's Department.	1925
4	4	Herring fishing in Ardglass, Kilkeel and Portavogie – weekly reports.	1925–1929
5	5	Provision for loan of suction pumps to farmers for use in drawing flax water from dams.	1926

[*Source*: Public Record Office of Northern Ireland, Crown Copyright]

Figure IV.7: Piece descriptions

A piece description in paragraph mode (Figure IV.7.1)

Level	
2	Letters to G B Lloyd from Thomas Stewardson
5	1863 Mar 10–May 2
	From T S at Philadelphia, referring to GBL's religious beliefs; Russell's 'North and South'; asks for foreign stamps for nephew; marriage of the Prince of Wales; blockade and the North's case in the Civil War; Canadian news; compares attitudes of the British in India and those of people in the South; postmark on a letter from Lloyd, relates comments on part of it on civil war made by a young Quaker. Restates his opinion on Britain's attitude to the United States and comments on the 'Alabama' incident. Mentions GBL's opinion of the Society of Friends' attitude; holiday walking in Pocomo Mountain; banking law, some family news, English and Irish immigration into the United States and prices there; GBL's belief in omens concerning royalty; revenue from land transfer.
	Good condition; available.

[*Source*: Birmingham Library, Archives Department].

160

Piece descriptions in list mode (Figure IV.7.2)

Level			
4	E/3/90	*Letter book 7*	1682–1685
5	f1	President & Council at Surat	1682 July 5
5	ff2–3	Agent and Council in Persia	
5	f3	Fort St George	
5	ff4–5	Bay of Bengal	
5	f7	Sultan Abul Kahar Abul Nasser, King of Bantam	1682 July 7
5	ff8v–9	Capt Benjamin Harry of the Kempthorne	1682 June 30
5	ff10v–11	List of goods to be provided at the Coast.	[1682 Aug 28]

[*Source*: India Office Records]

Figure IV.8.1: A vertically arranged set of descriptions, including group, class, subclass and item
Level

2

THE ASTAM DESIGN PARTNERSHIP, 1800–1966

Records deposited by the ASTAM Design Partnership, Gloucester on 2 December 1970 (Acc 2593), 6 March 1987 (Acc 5428), 12 May 1987 (Acc 5462) and September 1987 (Acc 5548). The records form the archive of the predecessor firms to the ASTAM Design Partnership, and were previously located in the attics of the firm's former premises at 17 College Green, which had been used by the practice since the 19th century.

History
The earliest architect to be represented ... and the firm has expanded, but the acronymic name has remained.

Content and organization of the records
All the papers relating to projects were originally stored together, as was common practice in Victorian architect' offices ... This arrangement seems unlikely to be the original order ... The papers listed below are known to be incomplete ... by surviving client files.

The following abbreviations ...

_ _ _ *** _ _ _

2.5	D2593/ 1	OFFICE PAPERS	
3	1/	*Private ledgers* Four volumes, titled "Private ledger"	1881–1932
4	/1		1881–1888
	/2		1889–1904
	/3		1905–1923
	4		1924–1932
3	1/2	*Clients' rough and summary ledgers* The rough ledgers record in some detail the expenses with which clients were charged, and the various stages of professional work charged for; the	1876–1966

161

		summary ledgers are of value only in bringing together long-running accounts. There is no system of cross reference between the rough and summary ledgers, although both classes are comprehensively indexed. Eight volumes.	
3.5		Rough clients' ledgers	1886–1966
		1	1886–1888
		2	1889–1893
4	3		1892–1902
	4		1903–1921
	5		1922–1966
3.5		Summary clients' ledgers	1876–1941
		6	1876–1881
		7	1882–1888
4		8 This volume seems to contain all accounts opened 1889–94; smaller accounts opened 1904–1921, and a few accounts opened 1936–38; the latter two categories being inserted in blank spaces left when the book was first used.	
Level 3	1/3	*Cash books*	1882–1942
		The cash books are of value in revealing much of the internal organisation of the firm. They show, how, for example, the proportions of the work carried out by each of the partners; and the names of the employees in the drawing office. Three volumes.	
		1	1882–1889
		2	1889–1914
4		3	1915–1942

[*Source*: Gloucestershire Record Office]

Figure IV.8.2: A class description as headnote to an item description

353SCH	*District Education Committee minutes*	1872–1903
	14 vols.	
	According to the board minutes 1870–1873 (printed series), p. 74, a minute of 12 June 1871 states that a District Education Committee is to be appointed "... whose special duty it shall be to see to the attendance of children at the public elementary schools..." This committee appears to have met regularly from that date as a board minutes of 10 July 1871 (printed series, p. 84) records proceedings of the District Education Committee from 12 June 1871 onwards.	
1	1872 June 5–1874 Dec 2. No index.	
2	1874 Dec 9–1877 Oct 10.	
3	1877 Oct 17–1879 Mar 19. Separate index. 353SCH 2/3a.	

[*Source*: Liverpool City Archives]

PART V
SPECIAL FORMATS

17

Introduction to special formats

17.1 This part completes the general provisions of *MAD* for setting standards for archival description. The general principle which applies to the special formats is that

(a) *MAD* rules and recommendations are intended primarily to control descriptive practices in general-purpose archives services. It is expected that archives services which specialize in the administration of materials in one of the special formats (for example, film or sound archives) will continue to develop or use specialized standards, often based upon *AACR2* or the ISBDs; though it is hoped that these standards will not conflict with those of *MAD*.

(b) The general assumption made in the chapters on special formats is that where groups, classes or items which consist of materials in one of the special formats occur within the holdings of an archive service (which is visualized in *MAD* as the normal situation), the principal finding aids will be framed in the terms of the general *MAD* rules and recommendations, and will contain a brief reference to the existence of the special format materials. A linked special finding aid will then be prepared to cover these materials at the appropriate depth, conforming to the rules and recommendations for the special format concerned. The special finding aid so produced will form a natural but subordinate part of the repository's finding aid system, all parts of which will be tied together by cross-references.

(c) Another general principle of the special formats in *MAD2* is that areas, sub-areas and data elements which exist in the main table of data elements are not transcribed into the tables of data elements for the special formats. If the special format does not call specifically for the use of an area, sub-area or element, it is not included. Despite this, any area, sub-area or element from the main table may, if desired, be imported into the structure of a special format description, at the discretion of the archivist.

17.2   In this section, rules and recommendations are given which apply only to the special format concerned. Each format has a table of data elements proper to itself, followed by models which determine the way in which data elements are selected and arranged to form an appropriate description.

17.3   *MAD* general rules and recommendations are not applicable to the special formats unless they are repeated in the relevant section.

17.4   *MAD* standard level numbers do not apply to special formats, unless this is indicated in the relevant section.

17.5   Contents of Part V

Acknowledgements
Sincere thanks are due to the many colleagues and institutions who have helped with the drafting of the special formats. There were too many to thank in every case, but we owe a particular debt of gratitude to the following individuals: Michael Bottomley, Graham Cornish, Jacky Cox, Mariann Gomes, Adrian Gregson, Andrew Griffin, Michael Hinman, Steven Hobbs, Ken Howarth, Nicholas Kingsley, David Lee, Barbara Morris, Paul Sargent, Joan Smith, Sara Stevenson, Marcia Taylor, Malcolm Underwood, Alan Ward,

Kevin Ward, Christopher and Margi Whittick, Bridget Winstanley; and to the following institutions: Bedfordshire Record Office, Berkshire Record Office, British Antarctic Survey, Coventry City Record Office, ESRC Data Archive, University of Essex, Greater London Record Office, the Guildhall Library, Hampshire Archives Trust, Hereford and Worcester County Record Office, Imperial War Museum, India Office Records, the National Library of Wales, the Committee of the National Photographic Collections, National Sound Archive, North West Film Archive, North West Sound Archive, St John's College, Cambridge, Scottish Film Archive, Scottish National Portrait Gallery, Somerset Record Office, Suffolk Record Office, Tyne & Wear Archives Service, West Yorkshire Archives Service.

18

Title deeds

18.1   Introduction   Title deeds are included in the list of special formats because they occur very commonly in the holdings of British (and some other Anglophone) archive services, because they have a very distinctive form which has been the subject of diplomatic study, and because in the past the presence of many title deeds among the materials in groups has tended to cause an imbalance in the depth of treatment within finding aids.

18.2   The deeds dealt with in this format are those produced within England and Wales. It may be possible at a later date to provide another section for Scottish deeds.

18.3   The use of this special format is optional. If it is not used, descriptions of title deeds will form part of the general finding aids, compiled in accordance with the general *MAD* standards. If this option is taken, care is necessary to control the depth of description which is accorded to the deeds within their group.

18.4   Title deeds have some characteristics of their own which influence rules for their description. These are as follows:

18.4A   *1. Original bundles*
18.4A1   Because in the past the reason for creating and preserving title deeds was the operation of the law of real property and the protection of property rights, it is commonly found that sets of title deeds are held together in bundles which were created by the

original owners and which, taken in sequence, demonstrate the ownership history of a property. Such bundles often have original binding tapes, wrappings or containers, and frequently also original numbering or coding which indicates the place of each item in the bundle. Single deeds which have become separated from such bundles may still display some indication of their origin.

18.4A2   In actual practice, original bundles often contain materials which are not title deeds, though they might have been brought together as a convenience to owners interested in defending title. Typical contents of bundles are:

abstracts of title;
documents ancillary to title, such as plans, sale particulars, insurance policies, solicitors' bills and correspondence, contracts for sale, financial papers, bankruptcy papers, valuation and auction sale papers;
wills and documents produced in the course of probate.

Where these documents are encountered in any numbers, the main description should appear in the general finding aid.

18.4A3   Original bundles may be linked together in an original system of arrangement, especially where larger estates were concerned. In some cases, for example in college archives, original sequences are preserved by using original or ancient methods of storage, pigeonholes, cupboards etc.

18.4B   *2. Diplomatic character*
18.4B1   Title deeds, especially those of early date (say before 1300 A.D.) have long been the subject of the historical auxiliary science of diplomatic. This study developed a technique for the analysis of words, phrases and composition in legal documents (originally 'diplomas') which served to illustrate some features of the society which produced the documents. These features were usually connected with the development of the law of real property, or with the structure of legal administration. Though nowadays the study of the diplomatic of early deeds is no longer at the centre of historical investigation, its techniques and findings remain valid, and a descriptive standard must continue to allow for diplomatic features to be displayed to the user.

18.4B2   A study of the work of diplomaticists, economic historians and archivists suggests that treatment of title deeds is affected by period and that the following periods can be distinguished.

(a) Early deeds (before 1300). Since these constitute an important part of the surviving documentation of the period, as well as displaying the development of important aspects of society, it remains necessary to recommend as full a description of the individual documents as possible. In particular, there is a strong case for transcribing significant phrases, and including full reference to all names (including names of witnesses) and descriptions of property. These documents are likely to be of interest across national boundaries.

(b) Late medieval to early-modern deeds (14th to 17th centuries). These documents demonstrate important developments in the operation of the land law, and the effects of these on the creation of landed estates, and through these on society in general. They may also be important material for the study of the formation or expansion of urban centres. In this period, too, there exist considerable quantities of centrally recorded versions of the deeds, in the form of enrolments. However, the deeds do not form such a large proportion of the surviving documentation as with the earlier material, and the development of particular formulations was in some respects more regular (although examples of local or aberrant formulations occur and should be recorded). References to the diplomatic form of documents therefore remain important, but it is not so necessary to recommend very full treatment of names or property descriptions.

(c) More modern deeds (to 1925). These become very numerous with the development of estate management practices in the 18th and 19th centuries, and the coming of sustained urban growth. Especially large numbers of deeds, including drafts and estate copies, survive particularly from the period at the end of the 19th century and into the 20th. The evidence they give is increasingly duplicated by alternative sources, some of which are easier to consult. The need for full descriptions of such material is accordingly less than with the earlier periods, and archivists may have appraisal problems where it is very bulky.

18.4C   Within local record offices, deeds are often of particular interest as sources for the history of houses. The indexing of local features and topographical coordinates is therefore valuable. Where a detailed treatment of deeds has been possible, much potential value for various fields of research has been revealed.

18.4D Because of these special features, title deeds present difficulties in connexion with levels of arrangement and depth of description.

18.5 Levels of arrangement

18.5A The general rule of multi-level description must apply: sets of title deeds, like other archival materials, must be described at more than one level. The complete finding aid should consist of macro descriptions governing micro ones.

18.5B If two (or more) levels are not required, only the macro descriptions should be given.

18.5C The function of a macro description is to record the provenance and general character of the set of deeds being described, with context and background. Micro descriptions with detail about smaller entities or single documents should be provided within the coverage of these macro descriptions.

18.5C1 It would be easy to envisage the macro description as corresponding to descriptions of the original bundles and sets of bundles as mentioned above. In the rules which follow, this is presented as one option. In other cases, quantities of deeds which have lost their original context, have been rearranged in the past, or have no surviving original arrangement, must also be dealt with. Macro descriptions must therefore be allowed as part of finding aids to material of this kind.

18.5C2 Micro descriptions contain more detailed or piece-specific information on the individual archival entities which are governed by the relevant macro descriptions.

18.5D In dealing with these levels within the context of the special format, standard *MAD* levels do not apply. In the context of general archives, bundles would be items (level 4) and the documents within them would be pieces (level 5). Finding aids which are confined to deeds as a special format may ignore these level settings, and use an independent system of levels based upon group, bundle and document, with intermediate sublevels as necessary: for example

i	Group	Source, context or provenance (e.g. estate)
ii	Subgroup	Original groupings, such as distinct parts of the estate or sets of bundles
iii	Bundle	Original bundle or sets of deeds with a common factor

iv	Sub-bundle	Sets of related documents within a bundle
v	Compound documents	Sets of documents which belong together or are closely related (e.g. lease and release with final concord)
vi	Document	Individual deeds

18.5E In principle, further levels needed may be inscrted.

18.5F These levels of arrangement and description are for use within the special format finding aids. These levels are not number-ed, though there is a data element for them (if required) within the identity statement area.

18.5G The general rule that any level of description may be omitted remains applicable.

18.5H Within the special format, *group descriptions* are essentially macro descriptions, and therefore aim to give the administrative and custodial history (within the format, termed context and proven-ance) of the archival entities thcy govern. They should conform to the general *MAD* standards. It is expected that usually these descriptions will appear in the general finding aids with a cross-reference to the special format. In other cases they may be repeated as a headnote to the special format, or represented by a shortened version.

18.5I *Bundle-level descriptions* aim to set out an abstract of the story recorded by the documents within the bundle, noting the significance and scope of original bundles or sets of bundles. They may indicate particular documents if these are significant, but in general descriptions at this level do not seek to deal with individual documents in any detail. Significance and scope may refer to legal developments, family or estate history, date range, topography or the development of land use, and/or dealings in the financial or labour markets. Recitals of names or places within deeds, or distinctive types of deed, may provide lists of significant value.

18.5J *Descriptions of individual documents or sets of closely related documents* aim to set out the diplomatic character of the docu-ment(s), together with content.

18.5J1 Individual documents may be described in a long (calendar) form, or in a short (list entry) form.

18.5K Descriptions at these different levels may be linked by headnotes or title pages, and the special format finding aid may include retrieval aids such as guides or indexes.

18.6   Table of data elements (Title Deeds)

18.6A   The following table gives data elements which belong to the title deeds special format. Where the general data elements are relevant, this is indicated.

18.6B   The general rules relating to data elements apply. In particular,

Any data element may be used at any level;
Any data element (except one from the identity statement) may be left unused.

18.6C   *Data elements summary*

Archival Description Sector
Identity statement
Reference code
Title
Term for level (group, bundle, document)
Term for diplomatic character
Name element
Simple date or span

Context and provenance area
Estate/property history
Source of original foundation
Names of parties
Places
Development of estate or property
Dates of significant events or documents
Custodial history
Archivist's note
Original arrangement and bundles

Content and character area
Diplomatic description
Technical forms
Individual or problem features (variants if copies; whether a forgery)
Language
Script

Authentication:
Seals
Signatures
Enrolment or endorsement
Notarial authentication
Original annotations
Abstract
Full date
Site, place, estate, parish
Parties: personal, corporate, family names
Recitals
Consideration, covenants, conditions, rents
Effect of deed
Property descriptions
Boundaries
Field names
Other names in the main text
neighbouring owners/tenants
previous owners/tenants
Warranty clause
Subject keywords
Witnesses and witness endorsement
Executed; not executed
Counterpart; part of indenture
Enclosures; plans, schedules

Conservation area
Seal conservation

18.7   Rules for the use of data elements
18.7A   *Identity statement*

18.7A1   The term for *diplomatic character* (applicable at compound or single document level) can be chosen from one of the terms in the following authority list. In other cases a term can be composed which summarizes the diplomatic features of the document(s).

admission
articles of agreement
assignment
award of arbitrators
bargain and sale (enrolled)
bond
common recovery
contract for sale
copy of court roll
counterpart
covenant to produce deeds
covenant to stand seized
declaration of trust
deed of gift (gift)
deed to declare uses (of . . .)
deed to lead uses (of . . .)
defeasance
demise (in trust, etc)
exchange
exemplification (of . . .)
extract of court proceedings
final concord
grant
grant of probate
inspeximus (of . . .)
lease (for lives, years, lives and years)
lease and release
letters of administration
letters of attorney
letters of confraternity
letters patent (close, royal etc)
licence to alienate
marriage settlement
mortgage (in fee, by demise etc)

partition
quitclaim
recognizance (of . . .)
release
surrender
will

18.7A2 The *name element* is applicable at group or bundle level. It should be chosen to identify the entity by using the principal associated name as a title. The name will generally be that of the estate, the family connected with the estate, or with the parish in which the property mainly lies, or the property itself.

18.7A3 *Simple dates* or simple span dates appear in the right margin as part of the identity statement. These should as far as possible be restricted to 4-figure year numbers, but at individual deed level should be restricted to year/month/day or day/month/year. Square brackets to indicate editorial inference, and '?' to indicate editorial doubt are permissible. (See Section 16.6.)

18.7A4 Complex or non-standard dates should be given within the free text fields, preferably the diplomatic description (individual features). These dates may include regnal years, feast days, uncertain cases and the supporting argument for inference in undated documents.

18.7B *Context and provenance area*
18.7B1 This area is provided for macro descriptions, and should be linked to the relevant entries in the general finding aids.

18.8B2 Estate/property history: the data will normally be entered as free text, observing the rule of information retrieval (see Section 8.4B). Alternatively, dedicated fields may be provided for names of parties, places and other keywords. The story of the development of the estate or property, like the administrative history in the general standards, is generally only suitable to unstructured text.

If free text is not used, a data structure may be built on these elements: source of original foundation, names of parties, places, development of estate or property, dates of significant events or documents.

18.7B3   The *custodial history* may consist only of a reference to the entry in the general finding aids or in the accessions register.

18.7B4   The *archivist's note* follows the general standard but should include a description of the sequence of original bundles, which may require a description of the order and place in which they were originally stored.

18.7C   *Content and character area*
18.7C1   The *diplomatic description* sub-area is provided to contain the special elements required for the study of diplomatic. It holds the following data elements:

18.7C1i   *Technical forms.* This refers back to the term for diplomatic character in the title. Although the title entry will normally be only a simple term of one or two words, in most cases this will be sufficient, and the technical forms entry can be left unused. In complicated or unusual cases a free text entry can be made, to allow supporting or explanatory argument, with appropriate citations.

18.7C1ii   *Individual or problem features* allows an extension of the technical description to cover additional features relating to the form of the document. A particular instance is the possibility of variants in the technical form introduced by way of copy; or the case where copies have replaced the original in unusual circumstances. If the materials are actually or possibly forgeries, this may be explained here.

18.7C1iii   The *language* entry should be made in the macro description where it is standard through a group or bundle. Variations can then be indicated in the micro descriptions of pieces.

18.7C1iv   The *script* entry may use standard terms such as Carolingian minuscule, chancery hand, secretary hand etc.

18.7C1v   The *authentication* set of data elements is intended to cover all the technical items which originated in the need to authenticate documents in early times. Technical terms can be used to cover:

181

18.7C1vi *Seals*. A full seal description can occupy a special format of its own, for which there are national and international models. MAD does not include a standard for this. The seals element of this format, however, can be made to contain any descriptive items which are required: size, shape, composition and colour; method of attachment; recto and verso images, and attribution; motto or inscription; skippets or containers; state of preservation.

18.7C1vii *Signatures* is intended for data on the authenticating signatures. Where the deed is an indenture, the identity of the signature is an indication of provenance; there may be other points of interest.

18.7C1viii *Enrolment or endorsement* is intended for data on endorsements which have a bearing on the content and effect of the document. Enrolment indicates if an official copy has been made and kept centrally. Endorsements of witnesses' names may preferably be entered in the abstract area unless there is a special reason for indicating them here.

18.7C1ix *Notarial authentication* should be included if present, following an established standard.

18.7C2 *Abstract* sub-area

18.7C2i The purpose of the *abstract* is to give a summary of the information contained in the entity being described. It is normally a free text field, but it is possible to structure it into dedicated fields to contain the elements which follow, if required. The list of data elements can in any case be used as a checklist, to ensure a complete entry.

18.7C2ii Site, place, estate, parish. Give a simple heading only. Fuller description of topographical data appears in 18.7C2vii. Follow local authority files.

18.7C2iii Parties: normally the parties are numbered by roman characters within round brackets: e.g.

   (i) Robert Herwarde, clerk
   (ii) William Hole of Crownley, esq
   (iii) Leonard Yeo, Citizen & Mercer and Armynell, widow and executrix of John Broke. These numbers may be used later in the description to identify the parties referred to.

Date: give the full version, including editorial comment and interpretative information (e.g. Old or New Style dates).

18.7C2iv   It is normal for names to follow the sequence: Christian name(s), surname, domicile, rank or profession. Names should be transcribed as in the original, abbreviating terms which are common form. Family or legal relationships should be transcribed. Square brackets can be used for editorial inferences, and ? for questionable inferences and doubtful readings. (See Section 16.6H.)

18.7C2v   Recitals (lists of previous transactions set out in the text) can be of value in that they can indicate transactions not recorded in original surviving deeds, or in parallel dealings. From this point of view they are valuable data. On the other hand, they may duplicate the information given in surviving deeds, or otherwise available. They can sometimes be very lengthy. Recitals are very valuable for the construction of bundle descriptions. In single deed descriptions, they should be transcribed in summary form if the data is otherwise not recorded; in other cases, their presence and scope should be indicated.

18.7C2vi   Legal consideration, covenants, conditions and rents mentioned in the text of the document should be transcribed, but this can be done in the form of a summary. Note special or unusual covenants.

18.7C2vii   In early deeds especially, all information about places should be recorded. In general the data in the original can be summarized, especially avoiding the repetition of common form phrases. Place names should be transcribed as in the original, but where their interpretation has been established editorially this may be added in square brackets immediately after: e.g.

  messuage and lands in Nytheragabwyll [?Lower Gabwell, par Stokeinteignhead]

18.7C2viii   Boundaries, including field boundaries, and the names of abutting tenants are of value in early deeds especially. The names of previous tenants and neighbouring holdings are equally valuable. Field names should be carefully recorded, as they are the subject of specialist study.

18.7C2ix   The presence of a warranty clause should be indicated in deeds prior to 1300. In early deeds variations of the standard form should be transcribed as in the original.

18.7C2x   In free text entries the information retrieval rule of the general standard (Section 8.4B) should be observed, i.e. all subject keywords should be included in the text.

18.7C2xi   Witnesses' names should be recorded exactly as in the original in deeds earlier than 1300, if necessary with editorial explanation: e.g.

　　Tedbaldo dapifero [Theobald the steward]

In deeds later than 1300 the recording of witnesses' names should follow local practice, but if given should preferably be translated into English forms. Endorsements of witnesses should be recorded or not, following the same practice.

18.7C2xii   Other notes could include any outstanding information not already covered. Whether the deed was executed, or was aborted before execution; whether the deed is the 'original' of an indenture, or a counterpart; any enclosures, added documents, plans or schedules. This particularly applies to inventories enclosed with copy wills, and plans with exchanges or partitions.

18.7C3   *Conservation area*
This area may be used to record the specialized processes needed for seal repair and conservation.

18.8   Models for description
18.8A   1.*Group descriptions (source, context, provenance),*
18.8A1   All sets of descriptions of title deeds should begin with a macro description which gives information on source, context, and provenance, and general data valid for the whole set. This description may appear as a headnote or title page, as in the general rules. It may refer to the brief description which appears in the general finding aids.

18.8A2   Such macro descriptions should contain an identity statement containing at least one of the elements for that area. Typically entries will be:

Reference code   Title   Simple date or simple span

Abstract: free text field
Bulk, size or quantity

18.8A3 The title contains an element for level. This is intended to provide for cases where a bundle or several linked bundles are being covered by the description. As in general descriptions, level indicators (group, subgroup, bundle, sub-bundle, compound documents or single deed) may be marked in either left or right margin, level with the reference code, but are not intended for use by readers.

Example:

Level:
  group
371/   *Estate of Summers Cocks family*   1597–1901
including manors of Reigate and Reigate
Priory, burgage tenements in Reigate.
[Administrative and custodial history,]

Subgroup

Burgage deeds
These cover most of the burgage tenements
recognized by the survey by William Bryant in
1786. For many of them the sequence begins
in the late 17th century, but for one in the
early 15th. Many original deed bundles were
found intact, or could be reconstructed. A
register of deed bundle numbers of Lord
Somers's properties exists [ref], and these
numbers were found on the documents. The
order of the numbers appears to be hap-
hazard, bearing no relation to the geographical position of the properties, though
adjacent numbers sometimes indicate properties bought in one transaction. There may
have been a plan of the borough on which the
numbers were shown, but this has not come
to light.
[0.7 5 m shelving in 10 boxes]

[Source: Surrey Record Office]

18.8B *2. Bundle descriptions*
18.8B1 This level may be used for related sets of original bundles, single original bundles, or individual deeds brought together because of some common characteristic.

18.8B2 The aim of these descriptions is to summarize the story documented by the bundle. The essential feature here, therefore, is the abstract, a free text field used to contain an account of the sequence of events recorded in the documents: acquisition of property, its passage from one individual or family to another, the administration of the estate, and its dissolution or absorption. The narrative may include reference to diplomatic aspects, and note individual documents of interest, but the objective at this level is not to concentrate particularly on single documents, but to give an overall view. Significant names of persons and places, and subject keywords should be given.

Reference code	Title	Simple dates
Bulk/quantity		
Abstract		

Example:

Level:
  bundle

DD/EV21   *Stoke St Michael*   1782–1826
    13 documents
    Paper mill at Stoke Bottom, described in latest deeds
    as "new erected paper mill and new erected houses in
    Stoke Bottom". This had been built probably in or
    soon after 1803 by Henry Fussell of Stoke St Michael,
    paper maker, on the site of a "late decayed mill with
    the barton behind of equal breadth and [the site of] an
    old stable", held originally of the manor of Doulting,
    together with a mill house and decayed or gutted mill.
    The earliest deed of 1782 adds that the first part had
    been leased for years and lives in 1733 to Ralph
    Stocker and describes the second part as a "new
    erected mill for grinding dye stuff". This latter had
    belonged to the Horner estate of the manors of Stoke
    Lane and Doulting and had been sold, probably ear-
    lier in 1782. The mill was gutted between 1782 and
    1795.

[*Source*: Somerset Record Office]

18.8C   *3. Individual deeds*
(a) *Short form*

Reference code	Diplomatic term	Simple date

Abstract: Parties
          Property, place
          Event or effect of document

Diplomatic features: Language
(if used)   Seal
                     Endorsement
                     Original or counterpart

Example:

> **Level**:
>   **single deed**
>
> AMS5859   Bexhill, High Street, mortgage   25 Nov 1812
>   (i) Thomas Christian of Bexhill, tailor & shopkeeper, and Arthur Brook of Bexhill, gent (his trustee for (1) below,
>   (ii) William Lucas Shadwell, and William Bishop of Hastings, attorneys at law and copartners.
>   Recites mortgage of (1) for £300 by (i) to George Robinson and John Piper, tailors and copartners, 11 Jan 1806.
>   (i) mortgages to (ii) for £450:
>   1. House to which considerable additions have been made by (i), once enclosed with a stone wall with stable buildings and land, once occupied by John Cooper, then Christopher Deval, then John and Edward Prior, but now Thomas Christian and Thomas Bean; in High Street, Bexhill.
>   2. 26 roods of land, formerly part of Butt Field, with house built on it by Thomas Christian, occupied by Thomas Coveney Markquick; bounded on S by Hastings-Bexhill road; on W by garden occupied by John Crowhurst; on N by part of Butt Field belonging to Arthur Brook; on E by part of Butt Field on which a house, now belonging to William Curteis, is erected.
>   (i) Dower of Elizabeth wife of TC excluded.
>   Endorsed in pencil "Osborn House, High Street".
>   Witnesses, William Thorpe, James Norton.

[*Source*: East Sussex Record Office]

(b) *Long form (calendar)*

> Reference code   Diplomatic term   Simple date
>
> Abstract: contains all information held in the document which is not common form

Example:

312/TY135 Confirmation of grant [c.1160]
(i) William Fitz-Stephen
(ii) to Gaufridus Dagulf de Toton', wife Sarra and heirs.
Land near Toton' [Totnes] which Stephen de Tunstealle
gave to Fulco and Basilia [William's sister] in jointure: viz,
a garden between those of Hugh and Mark the younger; 2
acres called Walcrot between the hollow way and the
castle; 3 acres and waste [mora] outside the walls between
the monks' land and the boundary of Little Totnes; 1 acre
called Dotacar lying across the said acres; 1 acre called
Vineyard, between the garden of William Gaidulf and the
river bank. These were given to Gaufridus de Toton' by
William de Mortona with his sister Sarra [the donor's
niece], daughter of Stephen de Morton' in jointure.
2 and a half silver marks in hand, and 2 gold besants to his
wife, Isabel de Lingeure.
Witnessed by Henr' de Nonant, Roger de Nonant his
brother, Guido de Britevilla, domina Isabel de Lingeure,
Ric[hard] her son, Guido Croc senescallo [steward], Henr'
de Nonant, Ric' capellano [chaplain], Joce capellano,
Benedict clerico [clerk] of Hurberton, Ric' de Nonant,
Robert son of Herbert, Abbot Roger, Abbot Rad'[ulfus],
William Crispin, Reginald de Westeton, Baudewin de Bac-
camora, Reginald de Harastan, William Crispin junior,
Robert Eustachii, Ric' de Camera, Rad' clerico [clerk],
Gaut' Camel, Philipp' Will' preposito [reeve] of Totnes.
Pendent seal lost.
Printed in Watkin, H. R. *History of Totnes Priory and Med-
ieval Town* (Vol I, Torquay, 1914), No. XXVIII, p. 97.

[*Source*: Devon Record Office]

19

Letters and correspondence

19.1 Introduction

19.1A Letters are included in *MAD* as a special format because groups or collections often contain very large numbers of them, or are entirely composed of them. In these cases, a special format may be the best way to provide a suitable finding aid.

19.1B Most groups contain some letters, and where this is so, it may be best to include the description within the general finding aid, and avoid the use of a special format.

Example:

Level
2	Papers of Dan Archer	1920–1965
3	Letters to W. S. Smith, 1789–1843	
4	J. Wallace's letter-book, 1850	
5	Letter, KBC to William Breakspear on social questions, 1790 June 3	

19.1C The special format for letters is provided for relatively or very detailed descriptions of letters or correspondence at item or piece level (levels 4 or 5 of the general standard).

19.1D The *MAD* concept of levels of description does not apply to the special format, which is provided solely for detailed treatment at piece level. Natural groupings of letters, as subgroups, bundles, volumes of letter-books, or files, may be described in the general finding aid system without using a special format.

19.1E   The multi-level rule (Section 5) operates in that contextual and background information should be supplied, usually in a headnote but alternatively in one of the forms indicated in the main sections.

19.2   Terminology

19.2A   Although these terms are not insisted upon in *AACR2* or in any other standard of general applicability, it is recommended as follows:

– the term 'letters' should be used where the letters emanate from one originator (individual or corporate);
– the term 'correspondence' should be used where the letters are between two or more correspondents, whether or not there are copies of outgoing letters.
– where the letters constitute the file of a recipient, containing letters from several correspondents, the term 'in-letters' may be used, but 'correspondence' may also be used if there are a number of correspondents.

19.3   Arrangement of letters is difficult if there is no original order. It may be necessary to choose an arbitrary arrangement. Indexes, either of correspondent or of subjects, or both, are likely to be an important part of the finding aid.

19.3A   Arrangement may be chronological by date of origination, sending or receipt; or it may be alphabetical by correspondent, or arranged by function or subject. Examples are also available where there is a dual arrangement: a main text section in which documents are lists in chronological order of origination, and a second section in which summary descriptions are arranged in subject groupings. See, for example, the *Transfer of Power in India*[1] series.

19.3B   Subgroups may be established within the general arrangement, where sets of letters arise from a particular function, or deal with a particular topic. Such subgroups should be marked only as headings, or brief headnotes, which break up what otherwise would be a continuous series of item descriptions.

[1] *Constitutional relations between Britain and India. The transfer of power 1942–7.* Mansergh, N. *et al.* (eds)., HMSO, 1970–83.

19.4 Depth of description. There is a general presumption that groups or collections of letters call for considerable depth of description. The model for this is provided by editions of the letters or correspondence of statesmen or artists: for example the letters of the first Duke of Wellington, or of Rudyard Kipling. Where individuals of this stature are concerned, full calendars for distant use are the ideal. Descriptions which are less full than these may be required, but very summary descriptions will be confined to macro descriptions which are covered in the general sections of *MAD2*.

19.5   Data elements summary for letters

Identity statement
  Reference code
  Title
    Name element
    Term for general description
    Simple date

  Archivist's note
    Arrangement adopted
    Depth of description
    Particular problems

Origination area
  Sender
    Place of origin or despatch (address)
    Signature

Recipient area
  Recipient or addressee
  Recipient's address

Date area

Subject area
  Abstract

Diplomatic area
  Form/type/genre
  Status
  Authority
  Philatelic details

Physical description area
  Material
  Condition

Access, reference and publication area
  Access conditions
  Citations and references in publications
  Publication of text, extracts or summary

19.6   Rules for the use of data elements for the description of letters

19.6A   *Identity statement*

Reference code
Title
  Name element: sender, recipient or subject heading
  Term for general description
    correspondence
    letter
    postcard
    note
    card
    telegram
    letterbook entry
    letterpress copy
    draft/unsent
  Simple date
Complex dates are entered in free text in the date area. See date area and/or archivist's note for details of which date is being used.

19.6B   *Archivist's note*

Principle of arrangement adopted
    See Section 19.3.
Policy on depth of description (calendar or summary)
    See Section 19.4.
Record particular problems.

19.6C   *Origination area*

Sender: enter uniform name if possible; otherwise use a local authority file or name list.

Place of origin or despatch: as above.

The address given at the head of the letter is not necessarily the place from which the letter was actually written. Letters may be written on paper with a printed heading, perhaps of a hotel or club, or business which may be some years old, or out of date. It is not always safe to accept data provided in the document itself.

Where accurate, the correspondent's address remaining constant over several letters may be important for tracing a route taken (i.e. an equivalent of place-dating for early medieval deeds).

Signature: Note the form of this, together with the signing off phrase.

19.6D *Recipient area*
Recipient or addressee
Note any unusual forms of address (such as pet names) which might make identification in other sources easier.

Recipient's address.

19.6E *Date area*
Complex or uncertain dates may be entered in free text, with notes as necessary discussing them.
E.g. on the Sunday Laetare Jerusalem 10 Ric II [17 Mar 1387]

The date used should be explained in this section, or if there is discussion, in the archivist's note. For example, indicate whether the date is the one given on the letter by the writer, the one endorsed by the recipient on the letter, the date of the postmark, or the time of the postmark.

19.6F *Subject area*
Abstract: following determination of depth (Section 19.4), include reference to all specific items of information contained in the text of the letter, omitting common form or generalities. Quotations from the original text should be given in double quotation marks ("").

19.6G *Diplomatic area*

A term for form/type/genre.
A term such as 'holograph letter' may be taken as the default.
Otherwise use terms such as: letter, copy, draft, notes, enclosure.
  This entry may refer back to the title.

Status
This sub-area refers to the relationship between the item being described and the originator's file. Use terms such as: typewritten, carbon copy, letterpress copy, transcript/copy/draft.
Other possible terms are: autograph, postscript, endorsed "Received..."

Authority
This sub-area is provided in order to give an opportunity for recording the manner in which the document is authenticated. Terms might include: autograph signature, proxy signature, signing

off phrase, etc. If the entry does not specifically refer to authentication, but to the whole document, the preferred sub-area is status.

Philatelic details
  Stamp
  Postmark
  Envelope endorsements or marks.

19.6H *Physical description area*

Material
Indicate the physical medium and any special characteristic. In the absence of local authority lists, terms such as 'international airmail letter form' may be suitable.

Condition
Indicate the general or special condition of the material, particularly if this bears upon access (see 19.6I).

19.6I *Access, reference and publication area*

Access conditions
Give details of any access restriction which may operate on this item. If the access restriction is due to physical condition, the preferred area is physical description (19.6H).

Citations and references in publications
Enter any relevant citations.

Publication of text, extracts or summary
Enter any relevant notes or citations.

19.7 Models for listing

19.7A Either paragraph or list mode may be selected.

19.7B *Example of headnote*

The function of headnotes as a form of macro description governing a set of micro descriptions is explained in Sections 5 and 6.

The letters format is essentially a micro description format, operating at piece level (see Section 19.1), and so requires to be governed by a macro description. This may normally take the form of a headnote, but alternatively any of the forms indicated by *MAD2*.

Macro descriptions should give, in addition to information on context, background and provenance, as much data as is common to the set of micro descriptions which are governed. This rule aims to reduce redundancy and improve ease of reference.

The headnote example is given here in the hope that it may be helpful, but does not form part of the letters format proper.

XY23/17   [Letters of]   *William Cecil, 1st Lord Burghley* 1575
Holograph letters from William Cecil, 1st Lord Burghley, to Peter Osborne, Lord Treasurer's Remembrancer, concerning foreign exchange, with particular reference to the grant to Burghley by Letters Patent of 9 March 1575 of the office of Keeper of the change, exchange and rechange in England in the Queen's dominions overseas and of the monopoly to appoint and regulate exchange brokers.

They explain the threat to Burghley's patent from one Hunt, who has been authorized by certain Aldermen of the City of London to sue to [Christopher] Hatton for a royal grant to appoint brokers, and the need for the Queen's confirmation of Burghley's monopoly.
From Windsor. 21 Oct 1575.
Paper, 10 sheets and 1 double sheet in guard file.

[*Source*: Guildhall Library MSS Dept.]

20

Photographs

20.1 Introduction

20.1A The special format for photographs, like the other special formats, is provided for the use of general repositories. Specialized photographic archives will continue to use and develop their own practices, though it is hoped that common standards and conventions will emerge.

20.1B General repositories normally hold photographs as part of groups or collections. In many cases these now amount to considerable holdings which require finding aids specially designed for their form.

20.1C The general rule is that information on the background, context and provenance of photographic holdings is given as an entry in the main or central finding aid system, together with a reference to the special finding aid for photographic materials. Entries in the main finding aid system follow the normal rules and recommendations of *MAD2*.

20.1D The special format is not intended to cover microforms.

20.2 Levels and background

20.2A The general multi-level rule (Section 6) applies to the special format photographic finding aid, in that a macro description giving background, context and provenance, together with information common to the set of descriptions covered, must be given as a headnote or title page at the beginning of the special format finding aid. This macro description should also appear as an entry in the general finding aids, or be cross-referred to a relevant entry there.

20.2B Outside the macro description referred to, the special format finding aid to photographic materials forms a distinct entity linked to but distinct from the central finding aid system of the repository. The special format descriptions are single-level, and correspond to individual pieces.

Example of entry in general finding aids:

QB16/2	Album of photographs displayed at exhibition (See index of photographs)	1910

20.2C For conservation of the photographs as physical objects, repositories may decide to keep these materials together. Archival order can then be preserved by means of the general finding aid (in structural order) and the reference coding system. It may be convenient to use a separate call number for retrieving particular photographs.

20.3 Depth of description
20.3A The distinguishing characteristic of the photograph as a documentary medium is that it is the representation of one particular event occurring at a particular moment. The interpretation of the image so created presents difficulties because background and context must usually be supplied editorially. Essential explanatory information must form part of the finding aid at piece level.

20.3B Descriptions of photographic materials should also give information on the technical process used. The technical processes which have been used to produce photographs in their various forms are complex and have undergone a lengthy development. Specialist advice may be necessary.

20.4 Physical shape of the photographic index
20.4A The special format finding aid for photographic materials will normally be termed the index of photographs, or the like. It is

expected that it will normally take the form of a formatted card index, or of a computerized database.

20.5   Data element summary
Identity statement
   Reference code
   Title
      Term for form/type/genre
      Name element
      Simple date

Content and character area
   Production
   Caption
   Contents note
   Physical description
      Material designation
      Dimensions
      Process used

Management information area
   Conservation

20.6 Rules for the use of data elements
20.6A *Identity statement*

20.6A1 Reference code
Generally, each photographic item should have a unique finding number, which should also (directly or indirectly) indicate its proper position within the archive of which it is a part. This reference number may include the original negative or job number of the photographer, but usually this information is better placed in the content and character area.

Give the call number or reference, if this is different from the archival reference code.

20.6A2 Title
(i) A simple term indicating the form, type or genre of the materials i.e. photograph; aerial photograph; transparency; negative.

This data element is used to give the user an immediate impression of the kind of object that is being described.
Example:

'Photograph of Mrs Jane Rochester, 1867'

Suitable terms include photograph, transparency, [photographic] print, negative, glass plate. The term 'photograph' may be used as the default, and so left unstated. More detailed, technical or explanatory terms appear in the physical description sub-area.

(ii) The name element. If possible, choose names from the persons, schemes, objects or events represented in the item. Otherwise, take the name of any object, physical feature or topic which may appear, or the name of the person or institution responsible for creating and keeping the photographic record.

(iii) Simple date. The date to be entered here should wherever possible be a simple year date, and should refer to the date of the event or object depicted, or the date the photograph was originally taken. Complex or deduced dates are better placed in the content and character area. Examples of titles:

xb12   Portrait photograph of Queen Elizabeth II, 1954.
          Aerial photograph of RMS Aquitania, 1940.
pr2/1/48 Party of emigrant children, c.1935.
84112

20.6B *Content and character area*
20.6B1 Production sub-area
Give the name of the photographer or photographic studio which produced the photograph, with the address or cross-reference to a description containing the address.
Transcribe the original negative or studio number.

20.6B2 Caption sub-area
Transcribe and textual or notational caption within quotation marks. However, original negative reference codes should by preference appear under the production sub-area.

20.6B3 Contents note sub-area
The contents note is normally a free text entry, without limitation as to length. However, a contents analysis may be used to structure the information which would normally occur in this sub-area; in this case, appropriate data elements would include:

– full date;
Dates may have to be deduced from the pictorial evidence, or from knowledge of the type of process involved, or both. Some evidence may be available from examination of the location of the photographic studio etc, or from the circumstances of the group's acquisition.
The reasoning behind the dating should be explained here;

– site, locality or place (specificity may be determined by general policy in the archives service: e.g. authority list of place-names, geographical coordinates); the appearance of man-made buildings or objects may help date photographs;

– personal or corporate names;

– events or activities, with explanation;

– subject keywords (these may be provided from an authorized vocabulary, or by reference to an established list of subject titles);

– cross-reference to information concerning the parent group, or to correspondence files on it.

20.6C *Physical description sub-area*
This sub-area provides information on the physical shape, size and character of the materials.

20.6C1 General:
Information about the origins and background of the photograph itself might be taken from internal evidence, the wrapping, the type of process which produced it.

20.6C2 Material designation:
Indicate whether the piece is a print, negative, transparency, or other form. Give the polarity: whether negative or positive. If the print conforms to a recognized type, give the technical term for this, using, e.g. carte de visite, cabinet card, stereograph, postcard. Indicate if there has been touching up or 'improvement'.

20.6C3 Dimensions:
Give the dimensions with and without mount. Standard size names may be used if relevant.

20.6C4 Process used:
Some suitable terms are given in the following list. Otherwise use a local authority file or a short description.

Positive processes
Albumen print
Ambrotype
Collodion print
Collotype
Contact print
Cyanotype
Daguerreotype
Diazo
Direct positive
Ferrotype
Glass
Photogravure
Salt print
Tintype

lantern slide
35mm slide
Glass transparency

Negative processes
Glass negatives:
  wet
  dry
Flexible negatives

Colour processes (Agfacolour, Joly plate, autochrome, Kodacolor, Kodachrome).

20.6D *Management information area*

If space is provided for management information, it can be used to control activities needed for the conservation, issue and return or any other operations on the material. Confidential information should not be given on a public finding aid.

The chief use of the area will be to record conservation work, the present and expected state of the piece, and special requirements for future preservation, e.g. production of a photographic copy at a predicted date, or the availability of a negative for reproduction.

The area may also be used to record copyright information.

21

Description of cartographic archives

21.1 Introduction
21.1A   Maps are often extracted physically in general repositories and kept in a map room or specially designated area, for ease of conservation and access. There are often dedicated lists of maps (or map indexes). [Map indexes are often themselves cartographic; *MAD2* does not contain rules for these.]

21.1B   Archival maps are nevertheless particularly dependent on the evidence of their provenance and context. Provision must therefore be made for recording these, and preserving links which may exist between the map(s) and their associated papers. Because of this, both the general (group) finding aid and the map index should contain cross-references and background information.

21.1C   In this text, the term 'maps' applies to all types of archival cartographic material, although the most frequently found type will be maps. Separate rules exist for architectural and other plans.

21.2 General rules for cartographic archives
21.2A   These rules and table of data elements are intended only for use with cartographic archives held by a general archives repository. Where there is no provision in these special format rules, the general rules of *MAD2* should apply.

21.2B   Archival map description may need to operate at level 3 (class) as well as at levels 4 and 5 (item and piece). Level 3 should be used to provide for classes of maps in a group; level 4 is used for related sets of maps which may occur either within a class or as independent items; level 5 is used for single maps.

21.2C The multi-level rule applies: sets of micro descriptions must be governed by a macro description. Macro descriptions may take the form of headnotes above the text of micro descriptions, or a title page or title page section in front of them. Such macro descriptions may be the same as, or may refer to, relevant entries in the main finding aids.

21.3 Data elements summary for cartographic archives

Identity statement
  Reference code
  Title
    Term for form/type/genre
    Name element
    Date
  Level number

Context, provenance and production area
  Context/provenance
  Production
    Surveyor/cartographer
    Caption/cartouche
  Archivist's note

Content and character area
  Content
    Date of representation
    Area/place
    Site reference
    Map reference
    Events, activities, purposes
    Subject keywords
    Sources
  Physical description
    Type
    Scale
    Projection
    Dimensions
    Support
    Medium
    Decoration

Management information area

21.4 Rules for the use of data elements

This section contains a fuller explanation of the content of each data element used in the description of cartographic archives.

21.4A *Identity statement area*
21.4A1 Reference code
As for general format.

An additional call number or reference may be needed if the cartographic materials are kept separately in specialized storage.

21.4A2 Title sub-area
(i)   A simple term indicating the form, type or genre of the materials. *AACR2* uses nine simple terms (atlas, diagram, globe, map, model, profile, remote-sensing image, section, view) with an extended list available if this is necessary (see physical description sub-area). The default (which need not be entered in a description which is part of a specialized finding aid) is 'map'.

If a term is to be entered for this element, enter the most specific term applicable, without going into detail. The term may be qualified by noting the purpose for which the map was drawn up e.g. tithe map, cadastral map. Ordnance Survey maps, or other maps which form part of a series, may include their standard reference numbers as part of the title if this number is a sufficient ready identification; otherwise these numbers should appear in the content sub-area.

(ii)   Name element. If there is a title given by the cartographer or surveyor on the map, this should be used, using quotation marks. If the formal title is inaccurate or insufficient, it should be given only in the content sub-area, and a supplied title given as usual.

In other circumstances, give the name of the geographic area represented. Where the map shows a village, town or city and the surrounding area, the name element should be that of the village, town or city and the details of the surrounding area may be further defined in the content area. Where two or more centres are shown, these should be named in the title if they are of equal importance on the map.

(iii)   Simple date(s). Give the simple date of the survey or (if different) of the publication or completion of the map. If the map was drawn up retrospectively this should be noted in the context and provenance sub-area. Other complex dates should be entered in the content sub-area.

21.4A3   Level

(See Section 21.2B, C) Levels of description should generally be indicated, as users will need to know where the specialized index refers to classes, sets of related maps, or individual maps. Level markers may be indicated in the margin but are not intended for public use.

21.4B   *Context, provenance and production area*

21.4B1   Context and provenance sub-area

Give information on the origin, background, context and provenance of the map or set of maps, including cross-reference to the general finding aid system.

If the map was drawn up for a particular reason (e.g. scientific purposes), the circumstances of its creation should be noted. If it can be simply stated, this purpose may be given in the type/form/ genre element of the identity statement, but otherwise should appear here.

Note any dedication which shows under what circumstances the map was created, if this does not appear in the description of the cartouche. These elements may alternatively appear in the content sub-area.

21.4B2   Production

If it does not appear in the cartouche, transcribe any information on the cartographer or surveyor, or engraver if this is available. Individuals should be listed in the order in which they were involved in the map's production e.g. surveyor, engraver, printer, publisher. Information supplied by editorial inference should be included in square brackets.

If there is a cartouche, describe this, giving its wording in quotation marks. Local authority lists may be used to encode decorative types. Alternatively this may appear in the physical description sub-area and this is preferable if there are several physical or decorative features.

21.4B3   Archivist's note

Include information on the relationship of sets of maps and of their arrangement in relation to the rest of the group or class.

21.4C   *Content and character area*

The content and character area has two sub-areas: content and physical description.

21.4C1   Content sub-area

Content information may be written into a free-text narrative field in paragraph mode, thus forming an abstract.

The abstract can be used to record more details about the place or location shown in the map. The rule of information retrieval applies: that is, the text should contain all keywords required for indexing or searching. For example, townships might be included as well as parishes; the names of mines and the company that owned them.

The abstract is normally a free text entry, without limitation as to length. However, a contents analysis may serve to structure the information which would normally occur in the abstract; in this case, appropriate data elements would include:

Date of representation or publication, which may not be the same as the date of the survey. The reason for this should be explained. Include the circumstances of the survey, if not given in the context and provenance sub-area.

Site or place; use local or national authority lists if available. Give map reference, preferably by a current Ordnance Survey map reference, especially if the place names mentioned on the map are no longer current. Give the territorial limits of the map.

Events, activities.

Explanation/description of any key or reference table or explanatory text or of accompanying material (if not already recorded in the general format description).

Subject keywords.

Sources: record any sources or documents from which the entity being described was derived. This may be particularly relevant in the case of cartographic archives which draw on one or more older surveys without acknowledgement.

21.4C2   Physical description

This sub-area is intended to provide for information on the physical shape, size and character of the materials. There may be a need for reference to the call number or location record.

The following terms for specialized kinds of maps are given in *AACR2*.

aerial chart	aerial remote-sensing image
anamorphic map	bird's eye view (map view)
block diagram	celestial chart/globe
hydrographic chart	map profile
map section	orthophoto
photo mosaic (controlled/un-	relief mode
controlled)	
photomap	
remote-sensing image	
terrestrial remote-sensing image	

Scale – give scale as a representative fraction if possible. If an inch scale is given, quote this, unless it is clearly inaccurate (and note the inaccuracy). If these options are not available, but a scale bar is given, this should be measured in centimetres or inches and calculated in terms of metric or imperial scales; this calculated scale should be placed in square brackets after the measurement.

If the scale can only be inferred from other evidence, such as degrees of latitude or distances between known places, a calculation should be made and the result noted e.g. n miles to an inch (calculated).

Foreign units of measurement should be translated where there is an exact English equivalent, e.g. pouce = inch. Note the original usage. Where there is no modern equivalent, state the unit of measurement used e.g. Scots chains.

Where the scale is not constant because of projection, this should be noted. *AACR2* (Cartographic materials) Appendix B, which gives 'Guidelines to Determine the Scale (RF) of a Map', should be used for this.

Give the projection: e.g. Mercator, James.

Give the dimensions: measured horizontally, then vertically, in centimetres to nearest half-centimetre, or inches to the nearest quarter inch. Dimensions should be taken from the marked borders, and if there is a margin containing a title, or reference table etc, these larger measurements should also be given. The overall size should be given for searchroom management purposes and may also be cross-referenced to the location record.

For a circular map give the diameter in the same way.

If the map is made up of several joined sheets, the overall size of the map should be entered, with the number of sheets.

The existence of inset or overlay maps should be noted.

Note the support or mounting – e.g. linen, tracing cloth, parchment. Note whether dissected, back to back/on both sides, whether rolled or flat (if this is different from usual practice in the repository).

Medium/technique: state the medium used e.g. charcoal, ink wash, colour wash, watercolour, black/colour pencil etc.

State the reproduction technique e.g. copperplate or wood engraving, lithograph, print, colour highlights, architects's copy, computer assisted etc.

Decoration: the following may be noted:

- colour used to differentiate parts of the map;
- decorated title;
- decorated border;
- cartouche: if this does not appear in the production sub-area, state contents e.g. title, and form e.g. decorated oval, unrolled scroll, pedestal etc. Describe or name the style if recognizable;
- heraldic or genealogical information;
- pictorial information e.g. people, buildings;
- compass cards/indicators e.g. rose, star, rhumb lines, cardinal points etc;
- any explanatory text.

21.4D *Management information area*

21.4D1   If space is provided for management information, it can be used to control activities needed for the conservation, issue and return or any other operations on the material. Confidential information should not be given on a public finding aid.

21.4D2   The chief use of the area will be to record conservation work, the present and expected state of the piece, and special requirements for future preservation, e.g. production of a photographic copy at a predicted date. The size of tables needed for consultation of the materials may be a useful data element.

22

Description of architectural and other plans

22.1 Introduction
22.1A This section is intended to cover the archival description of plans which are to be found in a general repository. The most usual types are architectural, constructional and technical plans, including engineering drawings.

22.1B Like cartographic archives, these plans are often taken out of their physical context, and are kept and used in separate areas of the repository. Their physical similarity to cartographic archives often means that they are kept with the maps, but the differences between them and maps are sufficient to merit a separate table of data elements.

22.1C Plans are nevertheless particularly dependent on the evidence of their provenance and context. This is especially the case where they form part of contract documentation. There may also be links with drawing registers or indexes, design manuals, specification books, etc. Provision must therefore be made for recording these, and preserving links which may exist between the plan(s) and their associated papers. Because of this, both the general (group) finding aid and the plan index should contain cross-references, background and contextual information.

22.2 General rules for architectural plans
22.2A These rules and table of data elements are intended only for use with archival plans held by a general archives repository. Where

there is no provision in these special format rules, the general rules of *MAD2* should apply.

22.2B Archival plan description may need to operate at level 3 as well as at levels 4 and 5. Level 3 should be used to provide for classes of plans in a group; level 4 is used for related sets of plans which may occur either within a class or as independent items; level 5 is used for single plans.

22.2C The multi-level rule applies: sets of micro descriptions must be governed by a macro description. Macro descriptions may take the form of headnotes above the text of micro descriptions, or a title page or title page section in front of them. Such macro descriptions may be the same as, or may refer to, relevant entries in the main finding aids.

22.3 Data elements summary

Identity statement
  Reference code
  Title
    Term for form/type/genre
    Name element
    Dates
  Level number

Context, provenance and production area
  Context/provenance
  Production
    Designer/draughtsman
    Caption
  Archivist's note

Content and character area
  Content
    Date of representation
    Subject or purpose of representation
    Site or place
    Personal or corporate names
    Events, activities, technical operations
    Accompanying material
    Other subject keywords
    Sources
  Physical description
    Type
    Scale
    Dimensions
    Support
    Medium
    Technique
    Decoration
    Special features

Management information area

22.4 Rules for the use of data elements
This section contains a fuller explanation of the content of each data element used in the description of archival plans.

22.4A   *Identity statement area*
22.4A1   *Reference code*

As for general format.

An additional call number or reference may be needed if the cartographic materials are kept separately in specialized storage.

22.4A2   *Title*
(i)   A simple term indicating the form, type or genre of the materials.

If a term is to be entered for this element, enter the most specific term applicable, without going into detail. The term may be qualified by noting the purpose for which the plan was drawn up e.g. contract drawings. If the plans are part of a related series, include their series reference numbers or codes as part of the title if this is a sufficient ready identification; otherwise this information should appear in the content sub-area. Use terms such as sketch, working drawings, structural detail, elevation, block plan, cross-section, drawing. The default is 'plan'.

(ii)   Name element.   Give the name or title indicated on the plan, where this is accurate and useful. If there is no such indication, give the name and type of the structure or operation represented, e.g. church of St Mary the Virgin, Merton; Ambridge church hall, roof beams; Garrett locomotive, boiler tubing.

(iii)   Span or indicator dates.   Give the simple date of the drawing or (if different) of the publication or completion of the plan. If the plan was drawn up retrospectively this should be noted in the context and provenance sub-area. Other complex dates or successive dates should be entered in the content sub-area.

(iv)   Level.   Levels should generally be indicated in one of the margins, since they will help in the analysis of the set of plans being described and in laying out finding aids. Users will need to know where the specialized index refers to classes, sets of related plans or papers (items), or to individual plans (pieces).

22.4B   *Context, provenance and production area*
22.4B1   *Context and provenance sub-area*
Give information on the origin, background, context and provenance of the plan or set of plans, including cross-reference to the
general finding aid system.

If the plan was drawn up for a particular reason (e.g. a construction project, a planning development), the circumstances of its
creation should be noted. If it can be simply stated, this purpose
may be given in the type/form/genre element of the identity
statement, but otherwise should appear here.

Note any titling or title block on the original which shows under
what circumstances the plan was created, if this does not appear in
the name element of the identity statement.

22.4B2   *Production*
If it does not appear in the title block, transcribe any information on
the architect or engineer, or engraver if this is available. [It should
be noted that the originator of a plan may be more important than
the project or structure involved.] Individuals should be listed in the
order in which they were involved in the plan's production e.g.
originator, draughtsman, engraver, printer, publisher. Include information on the sponsorship or control of the project, e.g. the
name of the client or firm. Information supplied by editorial
inference should be included in square brackets.

22.4B3   *Archivist's note*
Include information on the relationship of sets of plans, associated
documents, and of their arrangement in relation to the rest of the
group or class. (See Section 22.4A(i).)

22.4C   *Content and character area*
The content and character area has two sub-areas: content and
physical description.

22.4C1   *Content sub-area*
Content information may be written into a free text narrative field in
paragraph mode, thus forming an abstract.

The abstract can be used to record more details about the place,
site or structure shown in the plan(s). A term to indicate status, e.g.
'proposed' or 'suggested' may be included. The rule of information
retrieval applies: that is, the text should contain all keywords
required for indexing or searching.

The abstract is normally a free text entry, without limitation as to length. However, a contents analysis may serve to structure the information which would normally occur in the abstract; in this case, appropriate data elements would include:

Date of representation, drawing, or publication, which may not be the same as the date of the structure or project which gave rise to the plan(s). The reason for this should be explained. Include the circumstances surrounding the structure or project, if not given in the context and provenance sub-area.

Subject or purpose of representation: give details of the scheme, structure or project which gave rise to the plan(s). Use the original project title if this is suitable. Indicate the present state of the structure or site, or the effect of the project.

Site or place; use local or national authority lists if available. Give Ordnance Survey map reference if appropriate. Give the spatial or subject limits of the plan.

Personal or corporate names: include the name of sponsoring, financing, commissioning or controlling agencies, if these do not appear in the identity statement. Include the names of architects, engineers or designers connected with the project, if these do not appear elsewhere.

Events, activities, notable characteristics of the structure or project, or the specific technical operations which the plan(s) deal with.

Explanation/description of any key or reference table or explanatory text or of accompanying material (if not already recorded in the general format description).

Subject keywords.

Sources: record any sources or documents from which the entity being described was derived. This may be particularly relevant in the case of plans which draw on one or more older drawings without acknowledgement.

22.4C2 *Physical description*
This sub-area is intended to provide for information on the physical shape, size and character of the materials. There may be a need for reference to the call number or location record.

218

Type: An authority list should be used if possible. Terms may be drawn from the list given below.

Axonometric drawing, bird's-eye view, block plan, block diagram, blueline drawing, blueprint, CAD (computer-assisted design) drawing, competition drawing, construction design, contractdrawing, cross-section, dyeline, elevation, ground plan, landscaping plan, ornamental detail, perspective view, sketch, presentation drawing, publicity drawing, reverse blueline, room scheme, section, site plan, structural detail, tracing, view, working drawings, worm's-eye view.

Scale: Give the scale as a representative fraction if possible. If an inch scale is given, quote this, unless it is clearly inaccurate (and note the inaccuracy). If these options are not available, but a scale bar is given, this should be measured in centimetres or inches and calculated in terms of metric or imperial scales; this calculated scale should be placed in square brackets after the measurement.

If the scale can only be inferred from other evidence, such as existing structures or distances between known places, a calculation may be made and the result noted e.g. n metres to a centimetre (calculated).

Dimensions: measured horizontally, then vertically, in centimetres to nearest half-centimetre. Dimensions should be taken from the marked borders, and if there is a margin containing a title, or reference table etc., these larger measurements should also be given. The overall size should be given for searchroom management purposes and there may also be a cross-reference to the location record.

If the plan is made up of several joined sheets, the overall size of the plan should be entered, with the number of sheets. Indicate any revision or appendix sheets attached on the plan to show arrangement of a different option than that of the main structure or project. The existence of inset or overlay plans should be noted.

Support: Note the support or mounting – e.g. linen, tracing cloth, parchment. Note whether dissected, back to back, on both sides, whether rolled or flat (if this is different from usual practice in the repository).

Medium: State the medium used e.g. charcoal, ink wash, colour wash, watercolour, black/colour pencil etc.

Technique: State the reproduction technique e.g. copperplate or wood engraving, lithograph, print, colour highlights, architects's copy, computer assisted etc.

Decoration: the following may be noted:

– colour used to differentiate parts of the plan;
– decorated title;
– decorated border;
– title block: if this does not appear in the production sub-area, give any additional information;
– pictorial information e.g. people, planning views;
– any explanatory text.

Special features.

22.4E *Management information area*
If space is provided for management information, it can be used to control activities needed for the conservation, issue and return or any other operations on the material. Confidential information should not be given on a public finding aid.

The chief use of the area will be to record conservation work, the present and expected state of the piece, and special requirements for future preservation, e.g. production of a photographic copy at a predicted date.

23

Description of sound archives

23.1 Introduction

23.1A   This descriptive format, like the other special formats, has been designed for use in a general repository, and is concerned with descriptions of sound materials which are to be included in general finding aids.

23.1B   It is probable that no administrative system is based on sound recordings alone. Therefore, in a general repository, sound material will be found enclosed with or dependent on paper-based archive material. Some of this sound material will be archival (i.e. produced in the course of business and retained for business reference by an individual or organization); some will be collected material.

23.1C   An example of clearly archival material might be that produced by radio stations and record companies in the course of their work; these emanate from administrative systems and are consequently transactional in character. On the other hand, inter-view recordings resulting from oral history projects are a common form of collected material and they have more in common with collections of private papers, correspondence or research notes conventionally held by record offices.

23.1D   Commercially published recordings may be received in general repositories as part of an archival accumulation. These too may be described using the format, although the archivist may decide, as an alternative, to use an appropriate form of bibliographic description. Where commercial or published recordings with no archival context are concerned, standard *AACR2* bibliographical descriptions should be used, following the practice of the repository or the data provided by the publishers.

23.1E The *MAD2* format is suitable for use in the description of, among others, the following forms of sound recording which may be found among archival materials in a general repository and elsewhere:

- radio broadcasts
- interviews e.g. oral history recordings
- recording of events such as concerts, plays, conferences, panel discussions, meetings, debates etc.
- 'actuality' recordings (live recordings of e.g. demonstrations, riots etc.)
- recordings emanating from (scientific) monitoring apparatus
- 'masters' and other material used in the production of published records and tapes.

GENERAL RULES

23.2 Depth of description

23.2 A A full range of data elements for technical description has been included in the format though many data elements will be inapplicable to the requirements of a non-specialist repository. However sufficient technical information must be included in any description to allow for conservation, retrieval and use.

23.2B Because users can only have access to the sound materials by means of an appropriate machine, the accuracy and completeness of the content and character area of the description is particularly important.

23.3 Levels of description

23.3A The general multi-level rule (Section 6) applies to the special format sound recording finding aid, in that a macro description giving background, context and provenance, together with information common to the set of descriptions covered, must be given as a headnote or title page at the beginning of the special format finding aid. This macro description should also appear as an entry in the general finding aids, or be cross-referred to a relevant entry there.

23.3B Outside the macro description referred to, the special format finding aid to sound recordings forms a distinct entity linked to but distinct from the central finding aid system of the repository. We would expect the special format descriptions to represent level 3 (where sets of recordings are a class), level 4 (where there may be related recordings in a single complex unit) or level 5 (individual recordings). Items are series of recordings produced in the course of a project or activity and forming a physical unit. Pieces are single recordings, which may not be physically independent.

23.3C Sound recordings are usually extracted physically in general repositories and kept in a sound recordings room or specially designated area, for ease of conservation and access. There are often dedicated lists of sound recordings (or sound recordings indexes).

23.3D Archival sound recordings are not often self-explanatory and may be particularly dependent on the evidence of their provenance

223

and context. Consequently it is important to preserve links which may exist between the sound recordings(s) and their associated papers. Because of this, both the general (group/class) finding aid and the sound recordings index should contain cross-references and background information.

23.4 Summary table of data elements for sound archives

Identity statement area
  Reference code
  Title
    Simple term for form/type/genre
    Name element
    Simple date of recording
Context and provenance area
  Context, provenance
  Archivist's note
Content and character area
  Content
    Date recording made or compiled
    Purpose and aims
    Performer, subject, circumstances
    Fuller caption or title
      Creator of work
      Performer(s)/speaker(s)
      Authority by which recording made
        or compiled
      Participation criteria
      Copyright
    Subjects covered
      Periods covered
      Site or place
      Personal or corporate names
      Events, activities
      Subject keywords
    Recording
      Date and location of recording
      Recordist
    Physical and technical description
      Carrier
      Material
      Size
      Extent
      Duration
      Playback speed
      Other technical data

    Cross-reference to conservation sub-area

Management information area
    Process control sub-area
      Copies record
        Number and format of copies made
        Original recording retained/destroyed
        Processing carried out
        Cross-reference to conservation area
        Copyright record
    Conservation sub-area
      Previous history
      Repairs required
      Level of priority
      Routine processes required
      Other conservation data
      Cross-reference to administrative record

23.5 Rules for the use of data elements

This section contains a fuller explanation of the content of each data element used in the description of sound archives.

23.5A *Identity statement area*
Reference code

As for general format.

An additional call number or reference may be needed if the sound materials are kept separately in specialized storage.

Title   The title sub-area may contain three data elements:

(i) a simple term indicating the form, type or genre of the materials; generally 'sound recording'. A more detailed descriptive term, necessary for technical management, should be entered in the physical and technical description sub-area.

(ii) a name element, briefly identifying the principal subject, participants or project, e.g.

'Peggy Archer's recollections of the Second World War, 1985'.

(iii) a simple recording date.   The purpose of the simple date in this element is to help give a clear immediate means of reference. It will usually be a simple year date, but day or month may be added if these are significant. More complex dates appear in the abstract.

The simple date refers to the date of the recording. A date which is part of the subject description should appear either in the name element of the title, or in the content sub-area.

The simple date should be omitted if it is not significant.

Examples:

Sound Recordings of House of Commons Debates, 1983–1985
Bolton Sands Oral History Project recordings
Recorded dialects of South Yorkshire, 1969
Sussex Bird Song recordings, 1934–1953
Recording of 'The World at One' (Radio 4), 17 June 1987
'Week Ending' (Radio 4) 1983–1986
Cassettes of 'Aida' rehearsals, 1937–1955
Cassette of 'Aida' rehearsal at Royal Festival Hall, 1951 June 7

23.5B *Context and provenance area*
Context and provenance
This area is provided in order to record the context of the sound recording and its relationship with other recordings or documents which were
associated with it because of the circumstances of their origination.

The provenance of the sound recording includes not only the
circumstances of its creation but also its subsequent custodial history
and its transfer to the repository (though if preferred, this may be
recorded in the management information sector).

Circumstances of recording

Date: give the full date if this is not provided in the identity
statement.

The *purpose and aims* of the recording are given in a series of linked
data elements.

Give the identity of the creator or originator of the material or
project.

Record the authority, project or scheme responsible for the
work: title, statement of aims and purposes. Note important
features; e.g. if the recording was made for a specific reason not
necessarily connected with the material recorded in the content
summary e.g. recording of language or dialect, musical forms etc.;
where research use may be related to the sound, nature or style of
the recording rather than, or as well as, the information content.
Include information on the intended audience of the recording.

Record the criteria which were laid down for participation in the
creation of the work or in the project.

Archivist's note
Include information on the relationship of sets of sound recordings
and of their arrangement in relation to the rest of the group or class,
including special arrangements made by the repository.

Note the existence of any transcripts and their length in pages.

Note the existence of other finding aids to the recordings e.g.
indexes or lists of broadcast material compiled by radio stations.

23.5C *Content and character area*
The content and character area has two sub-areas: content, and
physical and technical description.

23.5C1 *Content sub-area*

The content sub-area is an abstract which contains data on the production of the recording, and its subject matter.

If the title element of the identity statement area is not sufficient to indicate the scope of the contents, a fuller or more complex caption or title should be given at the head of the abstract. This may be a derived title, with a note to explain the circumstances. After this initial sentence, the abstract continues with a summary of the content of the recording.

The sub-area is normally a free text entry, without limitation as to length. However, a contents analysis may serve to structure the information which would normally be given. The following structure demonstrates the use of the data elements supplied for this format.

The *subject coverage* of the recording is summarized in a series of linked data elements, as follows. The rule of information retrieval applies: that is, the text should contain all keywords required for indexing or searching. Authority files should be used if available.

Chronological period covered by the information;
Full or complex dates may be used, or a general term for period, such as 'the Depression'; 'the Cold War period' etc.

Site, locality or place dealt with or mentioned in the recording. Local authority lists should be used if possible. (The place where the recording was made should appear in the context and provenance area.)

Personal or corporate names mentioned in the recording; if not recorded with the contextual information, give the identity of the performer(s), the circumstances under which he, she or they were working, and/or the name of the occasion or project.

Events or activities mentioned in the recording;

Other subject keywords for retrieval or indexing.

Part description:

express a fractional extent in forms such as:
'on side 3 of 2 sound disks',
'on reel 3 of 4 sound reels'
and express the duration of the part as noted above e.g.
'on 1 side of 1 disk (13 min.)'

Location of part/item on carrier.
Indicate where on the carrier the subject of the description is to
be found. Use terms such as:

disk: side, band, cut
tape: reel, track, cut

23.5C2 *Physical and technical description*
This sub-area is intended to provide for information on the physical
shape, size and character of the medium carrying the original sound
recording (not copies). The general rule that any data element, sub-
area or area may be left unused, still applies. Much of this
information can be cross-referenced to the conservation sub-area.
The technical part of the description should be precise enough to
allow the materials to be played on suitable equipment.

Carrier: describe the material or object which contains, supports or
presents the sound recording. Use terms such as:

cartridge
cassette
cylinder
disk (compact, direct-cut, optical)
tape (magnetic, video [used for sound])
wire

Other carriers should be specified, with detail if rare.[1] The adjective
'sound' should be inserted before the type of carrier if this is not
obvious from the context.

Material/medium: indicate the substance from which the carrier (or
that part of it which actually holds the message) is manufactured.
Use terms such as:

Cassette: ferric oxide; chrome dioxide; metal particle coated.
Cylinder: brown wax; black wax; celluloid.
Disk: shellac; vinyl; aluminium.
Tape: paper; cellulose acetate/PVC; polyester.
Cross-reference to conservation area.

Size: give the size, capacity or length of the carrier (not the length of
the recorded sound).

[1] Examples are Tefitape and Amertape (sound on film); early magnetic disks; direct-cut metal
disks; early non-Philips cassettes. Also encountered are tape of greater widths than standard
quarter inch, and recordings with individual specifications produced by dictating equipment.

In the case of a cassette, indicate the total possible playing time; for a cylinder, give physical length and diameter, and (if known) total possible playing time; for a disk, give the diameter in centimetres; for a tape, physical length, spool diameter, or total possible playing time.

Cross-refer to the location record.

Extent: this data element refers to the total extent of the entity, which may extend over more than one carrier unit. Use terms such as number of sides, cassettes, reels.

Duration of recording If readily available, give the exact total playing time of the recording in hours, minutes and seconds. Give an approximate duration in hours and minutes if the precise duration is unknown.

Playback speed.

Disk: rpm (revolutions per minute).
Open reel tape (and wire): ips (inches or centimetres per second according to in-house practice).
 (Cassettes play at a standard speed.)

Playback mode.

Give the information needed to identify the appropriate machine or method. Use terms such as:

monaural ("mono")
binaural
stereophonic ("stereo")
quadrophonic

Give any further technical data useful for the preservation or use of the materials. Not all this data is necessarily of interest to lay users. There may be cross-references to the conservation sub-area.

Precise technical details of disk pressings are unlikely to be available or necessary; the headings given below relate mainly to tape recordings, though it may be useful to give technical information on direct-cut disks and other media where available and appropriate.

Additional technical data elements may include:

Method of recording.
  Use terms such as:
    acoustic or electrical
    analogue or digital

Quality of recording
Note the quality of the original recording before any filtering has taken place.

Make and model number of machine used to make recording.

Recording equalization standard e.g. IEC, NAB.

Machine settings e.g. Dolby B, DBX, limiter, (on Nagra) music setting, etc.

Recording speed.

Track configuration and recording mode.

Other recording equipment used (e.g. mixer, filtering device, noise reduction system).

Microphone details: make and model number; accessories (e.g. windshield, parabolic reflector (for wildlife recordings); microphone placement e.g. tipclip mike on lapel, crossed stereo pair, dummy head mounting, suspended overhead).

Other signal source e.g. direct input from house public address system; original recording played on <specification> tape or disk machine.

Tape details: make, type (e.g. single play, double play, or give manufacturer's reference number) and date of manufacture.

Manufacturer's trademark, catalogue number (including prefix and suffix, and, if considered of value to users) matrix number.

23.5D *Management information area*
23.5D1 *Process control sub-area*
Copies record
The original recording which came into the archivist's custody is not likely to be the one used to provide access. Record details of the archival copying process, including:

the number of reference or conservation copies made;

the transfer of the original recording into a different format;

whether the original recording has been retained or destroyed;

any processing (e.g. filtering) carried out.

Cross-reference to conservation sub-area.
Indicate as clearly as possible the copyright position.

23.5D2 *Conservation sub-area*
This area contains further physical and technical details not within the public domain. Cross-reference to the physical and technical description sub-area may be necessary.

Entries in this sub-area may apply either to the carrier or to the recording, or to both.

Describe the previous history of the materials, including a note of storage conditions prior to transfer to the repository.

Record the current state of carriers and containers, and note any repairs or conservation measures needed.

Indicate the level of priority accorded to the group/class or item.

Record routine processes to be carried out, including inspection, rewinding, cleaning, or the creation of conservation copies.

The conservation record may follow that of the general finding aids, including a record of the identity of conservators responsible for work, start and finish dates, the nature of any conservation activity, and recommendations for future action. A record of materials used may be added, and a record of any specific funding.

24

Description of film and video archives

24.1 Introduction
24.1A This section applies to both film and video recordings except where special features are indicated. In this text, the term 'film' should be understood as covering both forms.

24.1B The special format for archival materials with moving images, like the other special formats, is provided for the use of general repositories. Specialized film and video archives will continue to use and develop their own standards, though it is hoped that common conventions will emerge.

24.1C General repositories normally hold film materials as part of groups or collections. In many cases these now amount to considerable holdings which require finding aids specially designed for their form.

24.1D The general rule is that information on the background, context and provenance of film holdings is given as an entry in the main or central finding aid system, together with a reference to the special finding aid for film materials. Entries in the main finding aid system follow the normal rules and recommendations of *MAD2*.

24.2 Levels and background
24.2A The general multi-level rule (Section 6) applies to the special format film finding aid, in that a macro description giving

234

background, context and provenance, together with information common to the set of descriptions covered, must be given as a headnote or title page at the beginning of the special format finding aid. This macro description should also appear as an entry in the general finding aids, or be cross-referred to a relevant entry there.

24.2B   Outside the macro description referred to, the special format finding aid to film materials forms a distinct entity linked to but distinct from the central finding aid system of the repository. The special format descriptions are single-level, and correspond to individual items or pieces. Items are linked film or video materials belonging to a single title or project; pieces are single units of film or videotape. (If classes of films exist, the class description occurs within the general finding aids, without a special format for technical information; the class description may serve as a macro description governing the special format descriptions.)

Example of entry in general finding aids:

TS9/16 Films of launching ceremonies	1910
(See index of film and video materials)	

24.2C   For conservation and use of the films as physical objects, repositories may decide to keep these materials together. Archival order can then be preserved by means of the general finding aid (in structural order) and the reference coding system. It may be convenient to use an additional call number for retrieving particular films.

24.3   Data elements summary

Identity statement
   Reference code
   Title
      Simple term for form/type/genre
      Name element
      Production date

Production history area
   Producer
   Context//circumstances of production
      Contextual information
      Copyright

Content description area
   Abstract
      Date
      Site or place
      Personal or corporate names
      Events, activities
      Subject keywords
   Physical and technical description
    Physical character
      Quantity, bulk or size
      Quality
      Duration
      Technical character
      Sound
      Colour
      Form of print
      Projection speed
      Playing speed
      Format dimensions

Management information area
   Process control sub-area
      Copies record
   Conservation sub-area
      Routine processes
      Master copy made
      Stock destroyed

Repairs required
Level of priority
Conservator's name
Start and finish dates
Repairs carried out
Recommendations for future conservation
Materials used
Funding

24.4   Rules for the use of data elements in film and video description

This section contains a fuller explanation of the content of each data element, and rules for its use. Where no specific explanation is given, refer to the explanation given for the general standard.

24.4A   *Identity statement area*
Reference code

As for general format.

A separate call number or reference may be needed if the film materials are kept separately in specialized storage.

Title sub-area

The purpose of the title sub-area is to provide the equivalent of a main entry in a bibliographical finding aid, and to give a label which can be used in ordinary conversation, or in a preliminary guide, and which will direct users to the more detailed data elements which follow. Film and video archives which have been published will have a title in the bibliographic sense; nevertheless it may be necessary to extend this by reference to one of the data elements contained in the title sub-area.

The title sub-area may contain three data elements:

(i) a simple term indicating the form, type or genre of the materials;

(ii) a name element;

(iii) simple span or indicator dates.

(i) A simple term indicating the form, type or genre of the materials.

Local conventions and authority lists should be followed. Generally a term broadly indicating the type of material is necessary: e.g.

Film of royal visit

Videotape of dental operations

The term should be as simple as possible, and technical detail or complexity left for the physical and technical description

(ii) Name element.   If there is a title given by the original film-maker or producer, this should be used. If the formal title is inaccurate or insufficient, it should be given only in the content sub-area, and a supplied title given as usual.

In other circumstances, the name of the principal subject or event should be used. If there are two or more main subjects or events, these should be named in the title if they are of broadly equal importance.

(iii) Span or indicator dates.   Rules for general formats should be
followed. If dates have been inferred from visual evidence within the film, this may be noted in the production history area. If footage on one film has been shot at distinct and different times, the two or more dates may be given in simple form, and further explanation given in the production history area, e.g.

'Film of W I jam-making, 1963, 1978.'

Examples of titles:
'Video and film recordings of social and official events at
   Bolton Town Hall, 1934–1986'
'Karamazov Bros Co Ltd advertising films, 1923–1978'

24.4B *Production history sub-area*
The purpose of this sub-area is to record the purpose, nature and circumstances of the project or event which led to the creation of the film materials. It should include information on the background, context and origin of the materials.

Identify the organization or body responsible for the project and/ or the making of the film, and also the person or persons who actually made it. Preface each name or group of names with a statement of their function. Follow local standards and authorities in determining whether to include assistants or associates. Personnel connected with the making of the film may include:

(on production): director, producer, photographer, animator, writer;
(on performance): players, performers, narrator, presenters.

Include enough detail to make the nature or scope of the materials clear, especially if a specific audience or objective was in mind.
Note the place and date(s) of shooting.
Record the occasion of first or principal showing.
Record copyright information; if this is not to be public, enter it in the process control sub-area.

24.4C *Content and character area*

This area is intended to provide an abstract which will contain a description of the content, scene, event, subject or topic of the film, together with a physical and technical description which will allow the film to be used on appropriate viewing equipment.

24.4C1 Abstract sub-area

The abstract is normally a free text entry, without limitation as to length. However, a contents analysis may be used to structure the information which would normally occur in this sub-area; in this case, appropriate data elements would include:

- full date. Dates may have to be deduced from internal evidence
  (either from the images or from related sound, if any), or from the container or packaging, or from knowledge of the type of process involved, or from any of these. Some evidence may be available from examination of the location of the film studios, or from the circumstances of the transfer to the archives.
  The reasoning behind the allocation of dates should be explained here.

- site, locality or place (specificity may be determined by general policy in the archives service: e.g. authority list of place names, geographical coordinates); the appearance of buildings or objects may help establish the date of filming;

- personal or corporate names;

- events or activities, with explanation;

- subject keywords (these may be provided from an authorized vocabulary, or by reference to an established list of subject titles);

- cross-reference to information concerning the parent group, or to correspondence files on it.

Subject divisions within the abstract should be linked to reference points for ease of access. Reference points should preferably be given in minutes and seconds; this method is preferred to reference points in footage.

24.4C2 Physical and technical description sub-area
This area is intended to provide information on the physical shape, size and character of the materials. Sufficient technical detail to allow access to the materials should always be given. Subject to this provision, any data element may be omitted.

Data given in this sub-area relates to the original materials, not to any copies made in the repository.

General designation Terms may be selected from the following list:

film, cinematograph film, motion picture; documentary film, film compilation, film excerpts or extracts, trailer, newsreel or newscasts or newsfilms, stock shots, rushes or unedited film material, film out-takes or unedited film, film spot, stock footage of film, promotional or advertising or propaganda or educational film.

Carrier Give a description of the physical carrier of the recording materials. Use terms such as:

film cartridge, film cassette, film loop, film reel, videocartridge, videocassette, videodisk, videoreel.
Within a description, general terms such as film or video may be omitted if the context is clear.

Format dimensions
Film: give the gauge (width) in millimetres. Use 8mm, 16mm, 35mm or another width. If 8mm, state whether single, standard, super, or Maurer.
Videotape: give the gauge in inches. Use 1/2 in. Beta or VHS, 1 in 2 in.
Videodisk: give the diameter in inches.

Quantity, bulk or size Give the quantity, extent, size or bulk (dimensions, number, amount).

Quality Note the viewing condition of the film: good, poor, badly scratched etc. Note if a copy of the original has been 'improved' or changed.

Note the physical condition of the carrier if this may affect access to it.

Duration Give the total playing time in minutes unless the duration is less than five minutes, in which case give the duration in minutes and seconds.

Give the length of the film in metric linear measure or in feet. Film is measured from first frame to last, and videotape from first programme signal to last.

Projection   Indicate special projection requirements (e.g. cinerama, Panavision, multiprojector, etc.); and say whether anamorphic, techniscope, stereoscopic, or multiscreen.

Sound   Indicate presence or absence of a sound track by *sd* (sound) or *si* (silent).

Record any special characteristics, e.g. if optical or magnetic, or whether the sound track is physically integrated with the film or separate on a synchronized recording.

Colour   For black and white use *b&w*.

Describe a sepia print as b&w.

For colour use *col*. If the materials contain a combination of colour and black and white, give this information: e.g. '1 film reel (30 min), sd, col with b&w sequences'.

Give the system of colour for film, using terms such as: Technicolor, Kodachrome, Agfacolour, etc. For videotape use SECAM, PAL, NTSC etc.

Form of print   Use terms such as:

Negative; positive; reversal; reversal internegative; internegative; interpositive; colour separation; duplicate; fine grain duplicating positive or negative.

Film base

Acetate or nitrate
Cross-reference to conservation sub-area.

Projection speed   Give the speed in frames per second (fps).

Playing speed   Give the playing speed of a videodisk in revolutions per minute (rpm).

24.4D   *Management information area*
24.4D1   Process control sub-area
Follow general rules.

Special features include: Control of creation of working or backup copies. Note the number of reference copies made from the original. Note whether the original has been destroyed (e.g. in the case of nitrate stock), or transferred into a different format. Note changes, deletions or filterings.

Access controls, or restrictions on screening conditions. Copyright restrictions may appear here if not entered in the production history sub-area.

Loan record
This area allows for a record where materials have been loaned for viewing or reference outside the repository and the rules for general formats should be followed. When material has left the repository to be copied for conservation purposes (e.g. to be transferred from nitrate to acetate stock), this information should be recorded here and cross-referenced to the conservation area.

24.4D2 Conservation sub-area
Record any routine conservation work carried out e.g. copying of material for reference or backup purposes.

Include details of any repair work required, including transfer of nitrate stock to acetate or of any material to a different format (e.g. film to video).

Record any current conservation work to be carried out and its frequency.

Indicate a level of priority accorded to the group/class or item.

Give a cross-reference to the administrative conservation records of the repository.

25

Description of machine-readable archives

25.1 Introduction
25.1A This special format deals with computer files which are archival, and for which a bibliographic format is not suitable.

25.1B A format for the description of computer files as bibliographical entities has been established through the work of the Standards and Implementation Working Parties to the Computer Files Cataloguing Group of the Economic and Social Research Council, and through the work of the ESRC Data Archive, University of Essex. This format should be used wherever possible.

25.1C The *MAD2* format is provided to meet the case where computer files are created in the course of business in an administrative system, and retained for the purposes of continuing that administration; this material, conforming to the classic definition of archives, should therefore be managed as part of an integrated system of records and archives administration.

25.1D The format begins by establishing a definition of records and archives in the context of machine-readable files. The definition follows those current in the context of hard-copy media. Machine-readable records[1] are files created by electronic systems, readable by means of those systems, which are created in the course of

---

[1] It is to be noted that the term 'record' in this context derives from the literature and tradition of archives administration. It should not be confused with the same word which, in the context of computer operation, is generally used to mean a set of related data items within a file.

244

some business or administration and retained for the purposes of that business or administration. Machine-readable archives are those machine-readable records which have been subjected to a process of appraisal and have been selected for retention in an archives service or repository, so that longer-term reference and research values may be exploited.

25.1E An administration which produces machine-readable records in this systematic way is probably a complex one. It is to be expected that it will create or operate a recording system which consists of interrelated databases and files each of which has an individual structure and content. Where this is so, a descriptive system is needed which takes account of the complexity of the database, and does not treat each data file as a distinct bibliographic entity.

25.1F Though at the time of writing (1988) it has not been possible to examine an administration which operates solely or mainly through a computer system, it is not difficult to imagine that such administrations may or will exist. The administrative computing system of the University of Liverpool has been taken as a model, and is represented in Figure V.25.1.

25.2 Level of description
25.2A Like the other special formats, this one is drawn up with the object of providing for the needs of a general repository. It is therefore assumed that macro descriptions will appear as entries in the general finding aid system, referring users to a separate file of special format descriptions.

25.2B Group and class descriptions are given in the general finding aid system, contain no detailed technological information, and follow the general rules of *MAD2*. The special format descriptions which form the machine-readable description file are given at levels 3, 4 and 5 only. Level 3 (class) is used to describe whole related sets of files, which are usually seen as databases. Level 4 (items) is used for related sets of materials which form physical units for handling purposes; level 5 (pieces) for distinct and recognizable files which form the most elementary unit of arrangement and description, and which may be parts or components of items.

Figure V 25.1 A machine-readable administrative records system

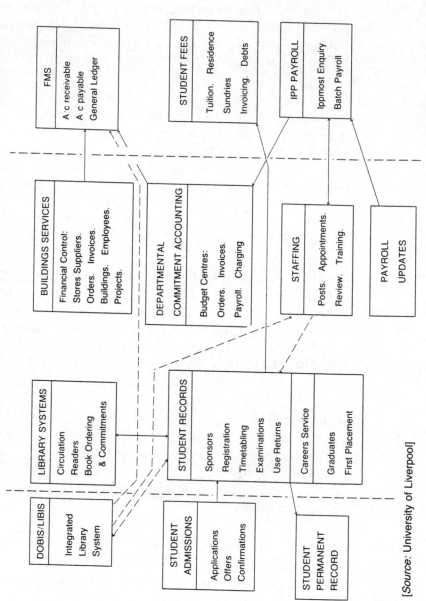

[*Source:* University of Liverpool]

25.2C For conservation of the machine-readable files as physical objects, repositories may decide to keep these materials together in specialized storage. Archival order can then be preserved by means of the general finding aid (in structural order) and the reference coding system. It may be convenient to use an additional call number for retrieving particular files.

25.3 Data elements

Detailed technical information is needed since the materials can only be accessed technologically. Conservation and maintenance also need to use and control technological processes.

25.4 Summary table of data elements for computer archives

Identity statement
  Reference code
  Title
    Term for form/type/genre
    Name element
    Simple date

Content and character area
  Production
    Aim and purpose
    Context and background
    Statement of responsibility
    Retirement or closure
    Access conditions
    Copyright
  Content
  Physical description
    Size or extent
    Medium
    Other characteristics

Technical description
    Memory requirement
    Language dependence
    Peripherals needed

Management information area
    Process history
    Updating
    Archiving
    Local access conditions
    Charges

25.5 Rules for the use of data elements
25.5A *Identity statement*
25.5A1 Reference code
Generally, each machine-readable file should have a unique finding code, which should also (directly or indirectly) indicate its proper position within the archive of which it is a part.

Give the call number or reference, if this is different from the archival reference code.

25.5A2 Title
(i) A simple term indicating the form, type or genre of the materials. This corresponds to the general material designation of *AACR2*. In most circumstances, terms such as 'computer database system', 'computer database', or 'computer file' should be used.

This data element is used to give the user an immediate impression of the kind of object that is being described. More detailed, technical or explanatory terms appear in the physical description sub-area.

(ii) The name element   Give the name of the administrative or database system which was used to create the materials, together with the name of the organization responsible, and whose records or archives these are. Indicate parallel or supplementary names or series. Example:

Merseyside Record Office accessions register.

(iii) Simple date   The date to be entered here should wherever possible be a simple year date, and should refer to the date at which the materials were compiled, or at which they were withdrawn from active use. Complex or deduced dates are better placed in the content and character area.

25.5B *Content and character area*
25.5B1 Production
This sub-area is provided to record the circumstances in which the materials were produced.

There are six data elements:

Aim and purpose
Context and background
Statement of responsibility
Retirement or closure
Access condition
Copyright.

Aim and purpose   Explain the aim and purpose of the creating institution. This may be a brief statement of the administrative function envisaged, e.g. 'database system designed for the central administration of . . .'

Context and background   Give further contextual information concerning the conditions in which the system was introduced.

Statement of responsibility   Record the names of institutions, departments or individuals who were responsible for system design, data structure, data capture or retrieval, or management.

Retirement or closure   Record the circumstances in which the materials were brought from current administrative use into record or archive management. This may be obsolescence or replacement of the system by another, or it may be the result of a management decision to take archival copies from an active system at predetermined moments. In the latter case, reference should be made to other related archival cross-sections, to the continuing administrative record and to the method used for controlling the extraction of archival data.

Access conditions   Indicate the conditions imposed for non-administrative reference to the materials.

Copyright   Include any reference to data protection registration.

25.5B2   Content sub-area
This sub-area is provided to contain an abstract, including more detailed or more complex information than was possible for the identity statement area.

Give a more specific description of the form, type or genre of the materials. Examples of appropriate terms are 'data file', which may be qualified by terms such as bibliographic, text, graphics, numeric; 'program file' (qualifiers may include terms such as operating system, program language, utility, applications; 'mixed file' (qualify as dynamic or static). Indicate the nature of the links between files within the system or with other files or databases.

25.5B3   Physical description
Full and explicit entries in this sub-area are necessary in order to ensure continued access to the materials and their conservation.

Size or extent   Enter the number of records in kilobytes (text files) or lines of code (program files).

Medium   Suitable terms are: magnetic tape, punched card, floppy disk (with size), cassette tape, ROM chip, ROM cartridge, micro-drive, CD-ROM, optical disk.

Other characteristics   Give the density, number of tracks, number of sides (disks), number of bits per inch (bpi), number of records per block (magnetic tapes), recording mode (e.g. double density, single density etc).

25.5B4   Technical description
Full and explicit entries in this area are necessary in order to ensure continued access to the materials and their conservation.

Memory requirement   Give the amount of memory addressibility (applicable to personal computers).

Language dependence   Give the software name, high-level language or code originally used, and indicate subsequent transfers or compatibility.

Peripherals needed
   Input: record the equipment used for original input. Terms such as microphone, concept keyboard, touch screen, light pen, tracker ball etc. may be used.
   Output: indicate equipment which is needed in order to achieve output from the materials; terms include graphics facilities (specific terms cover this), plotter, loudspeaker, printer.

25.5C   *Management information*
This area is provided in order to help control the conservation and use of the materials.

Process history   Record the process history of the local file or files, including processing carried out at the point of transfer to the repository, and the processing programme expected for the future (rewinding, cleaning, retensioning, checking, etc.).

Updating   Information is needed in this element where the content of the materials is to be altered as a consequence of subsequent accessions of related materials.

Archiving   Record the administrative system in force which controls the passage of active records to inactive, or the transfer of databases or files from active administration to the repository. Record also systems in use for security backup.

Local access conditions   Use the production area to record general policy on access. This entry refers to specific requirements of place and time, hardware or software installation, registration of users and other specific requirements for providing access once conditions of access are agreed.

Charges   Indicate charges applicable for services in giving access, including editing and copying.

MARC for archives and manuscripts

The AMC format as applied to the UK MARC standard

No cataloguing standard would be seen as complete unless it could be successfully related to the standards laid down by the public access electronic databases, and in particular to the MARC format which governs entries in these.

A MARC standard for general bibliographic descriptions has existed for some years. Over time, differences in national tradition and procedures have developed, so that the rules for MARC differ in the major countries which use it. The general MARC standard, though it is intended to contain a variety of bibliographic descriptions, and is therefore kept as flexible as possible, is not suitable for archival descriptions. This problem was overcome in North America in 1984 by the creation of a US/MARC format specially designed for use with archival materials: this was AMC (Archives and Manuscripts Control). With the aid of this format, very large numbers of archival descriptions were entered into public access databases, and both professionals and users in the USA and Canada began to accustom themselves to using this rapid form of exchange of data.

Since the US formats are not suitable for work in Britain, the programme of the Archival Description Project included the preparation of a draft UK MARC AMC format. This was done, and an outline of the format became available for discussion in professional circles in the spring of 1989. Copies may be obtained from the project team at the University of Liverpool.

It is hoped that this preliminary work on MARC AMC will facilitate forward planning in the field of archives administration.

The outline draft was written in order to promote the establishment of the AMC format within the tradition of UK MARC. It follows the US/MARC AMC format closely, and has been devised in the light of experience in North America with archival descriptions held in electronic databases.

The draft outline MARC AMC format, in the form in which it has been made available by the project team, sets out a full list of the various tags, fields and subfields, and indicates their relationship with features of *MAD2*. A fuller version, containing all the rules, definitions and examples which would allow practical use of the format, will appear separately in due course.

It is intended that the format should conform to every relevant MARC standard, as laid down in officially recognized documents, even though the document at the time of writing has only the status of a discussion draft.

Dictionary of technical terms

The dictionary includes only words which are used in a technical sense within *MAD*, and which therefore are to be regarded as terms of art within the context of archival description. For a wider approach to professional terminology, readers are referred to one of the authoritative glossaries which are mentioned in the bibliography

As far as possible, definitions have been based on the *Dictionary of Archival Terminology* published by the International Council on Archives in 1984. However, variations have been necessary in some cases because of the development of underlying concepts.

Words in italic are defined in the dictionary. Sources referred to in square brackets are cited at the end of the dictionary.

Abstract
In information work generally, a concise summary of a document, without added interpretation or criticism.

In *MAD*, one of the *sub-areas* of the *data elements* table.

Access (condition, state)
The availability of an *archival entity* for consultation as a result either or both of legal authorization and the existence of *finding aids*; access may also be affected by the physical state of the materials, or the need to conserve them.

Access, to (verb)
The act of obtaining *access* to a document; the act of referring to an *archival entity*.

Access points
This term is used in *AACR2* to mean a *keyword* or *entry* which would serve as the heading to an *index* card; this card would then serve as an additional description of the materials it refers to. The term is not directly useful in archives administration, but is used in *MAD* to mean a part of the *finding aid system* at which a user can begin a search for relevant documents.

Accession (noun)
An acquisition; an assembly of materials taken into custody at one time.

Accession, to (verb)
To record the formal acceptance into custody of an *accession*.

Accession number (code, or reference)
The number or *code* allocated to an *accession* in order to identify it for administrative purposes. This number is normally recorded in an accession register and in practice often serves to identify a *group* or *collection* within a *repository*, at least until that group has been fully processed. In some cases accession numbers remain permanently in use as identifiers of groups: in this case the preferred term would be *reference code*.

Accretion
Use *accrual*.

Accrual
An acquisition of materials which belong to a *group* or *class* already in the custody of a *repository*.

Analytical inventory
Use *list* or *handlist*.

Archival entity
In *MAD*, this term means any unit of an archival accumulation which is under consideration at the time. The term can indicate such a unit at any *level* or size: for example, it can mean a *group*, *subgroup*, *class*, *item* or *piece*, or any temporary grouping of any of these.

Archival relationships, archival order
The relationships between components of an archival entity arising from the original system under which they were created, the order

256

or sequence of components of an archive which demonstrate this system.

Archive

A general term which in some contexts can be used in place of *archival entity* to indicate any unit of an archival accumulation which has to be considered separately for management or descriptive action; also used as a synonym for *collection*, for which it is a preferred term.

Archive group

In *MAD1* this term was used for *management group*, which is now the preferred term.

Archives

(a) A *repository*, which is the preferred term;
(b) A general term for the materials held within a repository.
See also *papers, records*. May be used as an element in the title *sub-area*, to indicate the materials which resulted from the business operations of the originating body.
For definition see Section 1.1A.

Archives service

In *MAD*, any organization, for example a *record office*, which is responsible for the management of archives. The term is broader than *repository*, which refers to an archives service only in its aspect of the holder or custodian of materials.

Area

In *MAD*, which takes the usage from *AACR2*, a collection of related *data elements* which together provide an aspect of the description of an *archival entity*.

Arrangement

The intellectual and physical operations involved in the analysis and organization of archives: the equivalent in archives administration to *classification* in librarianship. Archives are arranged in relation to other related archives, and not in relation to a pre-established *index* of concepts.

Authority list

A list of terms which is authorized by a controlling body for use in archival or bibliographic descriptions. An example is a list of parishes drawn up by a *record office*; this list establishes correct spellings, and determines the headings or labels under which the names of townships or hamlets will be indexed. In other cases, authority lists contain subject keywords arranged in logical order, and so providing *access points*.

Bibliographic description
The description of a bibliographic item, in conformity with the rules currently in force for this type of description (at present *AACR2*, *ISBD* etc.). The term should if possible be avoided for archives, except where (as in entries in online databases which refer to archival materials) descriptions are specially written to conform to bibliographical standards.

Box
A storage and retrieval unit consisting of a rigid container, provided by the *repository*, to contain a number of *items* or *pieces*, whether or not related by content or function.

Bundle
A storage and retrieval unit consisting of a number of *pieces*, whether or not related by content or function, normally tied together by string, tape etc. A bundle may be 'original', or formed by arrangement.

Calendar
A *list*, usually in chronological order, containing very full summaries of individual documents in the same *class* or of a specified kind from a number of sources, giving all content and material information valuable to the user. A calendar differs from a transcript only in that common form phrases are summarized or omitted. Calendars are intended to serve as *surrogates* for the originals they refer to, especially for remote users.

Call number
See *reference code*; a *code* which identifies an *item* for the purpose of retrieval.

Catalogue
A set of *archival descriptions* which includes descriptions of all the components of one or more related *management groups*, *groups* or *collections* at all the different *levels* used, and with an index. The concept is explained at Section 6.3.

Checklist
A *list*, usually of an individual *accession*, prepared by the transferring agency for purposes of identification and physical control.

Citation
1. 'A note referring to a work, or an archival document, from which a passage is quoted or to some source of authority for a statement or proposition' [Evans, 1974].
2. A brief *bibliographic* or *archival description* appearing in a secondary work or *list*.
There are standards for the form of citations (BS5605/1978 and BS6371/1983).

Class
Level 3 of archival *arrangement*. In Britain, use for *series*, which is the international term. See Section 4.6E.

Class list
A list of *classes* within a *group*: this is the preferred usage. It is also used to mean a list of *items* in a *class* in numerical order with minimum detail.

Classification
The arrangement of materials in accordance with a pre-existing *scheme* or *index* of concepts or a filing system; the arrangement may be conceptual rather than physical, and the materials may include *keywords* or *index* entries.

Classification scheme
A pattern or arrangement of concepts, setting out the relationship of one to another, in any field of knowledge, or, frequently, in the universe of knowledge. In archives administration, there are classification schemes covering *groups* which recur in different places.

Code
See *reference code*.

Collection
1. Equivalent in a manuscript library to a *group*. See Section 4.6C.
2. An artificial accumulation of materials related to a single theme, interest, type of document or person, or compiled by an individual.

Collections
Use *holdings*: all the materials acquired or held by a *repository*.

Composite class
A *class* which has been formed during the analysis and *arrangement* of a *group*, which does not derive from any original system in the creating organization but which for practical purposes brings together sets of documents which have some common characteristic. The concept is discussed in Section 4.6E3.

Concordance
A list of terms occurring in a *document*, arranged alphabetically or in accordance with a *classification scheme*.

Container
'Any housing for an *item*, a group of items, or part of an item which is physically separable from the material housed.' [ISBD(NBM), p. 2.] See also *box, bundle, folder*.

Data
The information which is written into a *field*; the specific information which corresponds to a *data element*; the information which is written into an *area* in an archival description.

Data element
In *MAD*, the basic unit of information in the structured table of data elements. The elements in the table are structured into sectors, *areas* and *sub-areas*. See Sections 10–12.

Dedicated field
A *field* whose function, content and (usually) length, are strictly defined by the *file* or *finding aid* system it is part of, as opposed to one (e.g. *free text*) which has no restriction on its form, content or length.

Depth of description
In *MAD* this means the amount of detail which is to be included in a description; the fullness of a description. Rules for it are in Section 8.

Describe, to
The act of preparing *finding aids* to facilitate control and consultation of *holdings*.

Description
A component of a *representation file*.

Descriptive inventory
Use *list*.

Descriptive list
The preferred term is *list*, although the term, qualified in this way, suggests a list with greater *depth of description* than would be normal.

Document
A single *archive, record* or *manuscript* entity: usually a physically indivisible entity; a *piece*.

Dossier
A set of *documents* in a *folder*, placed there in accordance with an administrative system; often applied to case files or particular instance papers. An equivalent term is *file*, but this cannot be made the preferred term because of possible confusion with other meanings.

Field
'A subdivision of a *record* containing a unit of *data.*'[ICA/ADP 1983, p. 17.]
See also *dedicated field, free text field, record*.

File (noun)
1. 'An accumulation of records maintained in a predetermined physical arrangement.' [Evans, p. 422.] 'A set of related records capable of being processed as a unit.' [ICA/ADP, p. 17]. This usage originated in computing, but is applicable to normal archival management.

2. A set of related *data* items with a common title and purpose. See also *representation file*.

3. Synonym for *dossier*, which because of possible confusion with (1) and (2) must be the preferred term. See also *folder*.

File (verb)
1. To place *documents* in a predetermined location.
2. To store related *data* items so that they can be retrieved.

Finding aid
The broadest term to cover any *description* or means of reference generated by an *archives service* in the course of establishing administrative or intellectual control over its *holdings*.

Finding aid system
Defined in Section 3. The system which results from linking together all the different *finding aids* produced and used by a *repository*.

Finding list
Use *finding aid* for more general applications, *list* for more specific ones. [Society of Archivists, p. 1]

Folder
A folded sheet of paper or card serving as a cover for a set of related *documents*. See also *dossier*.

Fonds
Otherwise *fonds d'archives*. In Canada, equivalent to *group*, which is the preferred term. This French word was popularized by Jenkinson, 1965, pp. 18, 100–101) because it recalled the principle of
'respect des fonds' in archival arrangement.

Format (noun)
The organization of *data*, especially in the output or final version of a descriptive system. Where it refers to the shape of text on a page, the preferred term is *layout*. Also the physical appearance, technical character or size of materials, especially in the context of *special formats*.

Format (verb)
The act of arranging *data* into a specified format, or creating a page *layout*.

Free text field
See *dedicated field, field*.

Group
Defined at Section 4.6C. See also *management group* (British usage); *record group* (American usage). In *MAD*, used to mean the archives of an independent or distinguishable originating unit or agency. In some circumstances equivalent to *collection*.

Guide
A *finding aid* which provides a general account of all or part of the *holdings* of a *repository*. A *paragraph mode* set of related *macro descriptions*. Also used to mean a similar set of descriptions of materials dealing with a particular subject.

Handbook
Equivalent to *topical guide*, with the implication that it has been published in book form.

Handlist
A *finding aid* which contains descriptions of a set of a particular type of archive (e.g. enclosure awards). Handlists are sometimes multi-institutional.

Headnote
In *MAD*, a *macro description* which appears directly above a set of related *micro descriptions*. See Section 6.

Higher-level description
This term is used in *MAD1* to mean *macro description*, which is the preferred term.

Holdings
A general term to signify the totality of the material in the custody of an *archives service*, or a distinct part of it.

Index
An ordered list of terms, *keywords* or concepts contained in a set of archival descriptions, or in a *file* or *document*, together with pointers to the locations for those terms, keywords or concepts. See also *vocabulary, thesaurus, classification schemes*.

Information retrieval
The process of identifying *data* and the retrieval of the *documents* which contain it.

Inventory
Synonymous with *list*, which is the preferred term.

Item
In *MAD* the physical unit of handling and retrieval, in archives management. 'A *document*, a group of documents or a part of a

document in any physical form, considered as an entity and as such forming the basis for a single bibliographic description.' [ISBD(NBM), p. 2. See also Evans, p. 424.]

Keyword
'Each of the significant words in a string used as lead terms in an index' [ICA/ADP, p. 19]. More widely, any term capable of being used to identify information in an *index* or in a *search*.

Layout
The shape of text on a page: use for *format*, in this sense.

Levels of description
See Section 4.

List
An enumeration of a set of archives; the basic *finding aid* for *micro description*. Use for *inventory*.

List mode
See Section 7. One of the two principal *modes* or styles of setting out archival descriptions, characterized by short fields, little connected text, in tabulated columns.

Location index
A finding aid to control and locate *holdings*. Where the *index* format is not a strong characteristic, use *shelflist*.

Lower-level description
This term was used in *MAD1* to mean *micro description*, which is the preferred term.

Macro description
Defined in Section 5. A description which gives information on the background, context and provenance of a set of related archival entities, the descriptions of which it governs. In *MAD1* the term *higher-level description* was used, but because of ambiguities which resulted, macro description is now the preferred term.

Main entry
In *AACR2*, the complete catalogue entry for a bibliographic item, presented in the form by which the entity is to be uniformly

identified and cited. The concept is not entirely relevant to *MAD*, but if used would mean the *representation* of an archival entity in the principal (or structural) representation file.

Management group
Defined in Section 4.6B. In *MAD1* the term *archive group* was used, but because of ambiguities which resulted, management group is now the preferred term.

Manuscript
See Section 1.1B.

Manuscript group
Use *group* or *collection*.

Micro description
Defined in Section 5. Descriptions of the individual components of an *archival entity*, which appear below and are governed by, a *macro description*. In *MAD1* the term *lower-level description* was used, but because of ambiguities which resulted, the preferred term is now this one.

Modes of listing
Defined in Section 7. In *MAD* there are two modes, or general styles, into which *finding aids* can be *formatted*: *list mode* and *paragraph mode*.

Moral defence
Term coined by Sir Hilary Jenkinson (see his *Manual*, 1965 ed., p. 83) to summarize the professional duties of archivists in safeguarding the integrity and authenticity of the archives in their care.

Paragraph mode
Defined in Section 7. One of the two principal *modes* or styles of setting out archival descriptions, characterized by blocks of text arranged (in paragraphs) down the page.

Papers
'A natural accumulation of personal and family materials.' [Evans, p. 426]; personal, family and estate archives. The term may be used as an element in the title *sub-area*.

Piece
The basic single, indivisible unit in an archival entity. 'A discrete object or individual member of a class or group . . .' [Evans, p. 427]. Pieces may be free-standing, but if they are bound together by any physical means, the pieces within the unit so formed are an *item*.

Preliminary list
See *summary list*.

Record(s)
1. Recorded information or documents, regardless of form or medium, created or received and maintained by a person or an agency in pursuance of business.

2. In computing, a record is an assembly of related items of *data* treated as a unit; the basic component of a *file*; [ICA/ADP, p. 24]: by extension, the description of one archival entity within a set.

Record office
In British usage, an *archives service* or *repository*, which are the preferred terms where the service or the physical custody, respectively, are intended.

Reference code
The symbols, usually alphanumeric, which identify an *archival entity*. Reference codes are one of the *data elements* in the identity statement, one of the *areas* in the table of data elements. See Section 9.10.

Register
A chronological record of actions taken in regard to the administration of *archives* or of a *repository*.

Repertory
Use *guide, list, catalogue*.

Repository
An *archives service*, a manuscript library, or any agency which operates as such, considered as the physical and moral custodian of archival material.

Representation
In *MAD* a description considered as something which stands in

place of the original for certain purposes. The concept is discussed in Section 3, and is important for the design of *finding aids*.

Representation file
See Section 3. The assembly of *representations*, components of a *finding aid system*.

Schedule
In records management, a list of record types giving retention periods. Otherwise, use *list*.

Scheme
See *classification scheme*.

Search
The act of a user seeking for information contained in archival materials, or in *finding aids*. *MAD* discusses searching strategies at Section 9.6.

Series
International usage for *class*, which is the preferred term.

Selective list
A *list* which contains only selected *data* items; may be used as a *subject-based finding aid*.

Shelf list
A list of the holdings in a *repository* arranged in order of the contents of each shelf. See also *location index*.

Special formats
In *MAD* types of archival material which call for special treatment in description.

Structural finding aid
A *finding aid* which is arranged in an order which reflects the original system of the creating organization. The concept is discussed at Section 3.6.

Sub-area
A group of related *data elements*, part of an *area* within an archival description.

Subgroup
Defined in Section 4.6D. A body of *archives* within a *group*, usually those of a subordinate administrative unit, but sometimes those of a particular function.

Subject-based finding aid
A *finding aid* which includes only descriptions of *archival entities* which have been chosen because they deal with a particular subject.

Subseries
Use *subclass*.

Summary list
The term may be needed in *repositories* where listing is done in two stages, but in general the preferred term is *list*.

Summary
'A preliminary guide to the holdings of a repository, generally lacking in descriptive detail regarding the informational content of groups, subgroups and series [classes]' [Evans, p. 431]. Use *guide*.

Surrogate
A *representation* which can be used as an alternative to the original. See *calendar*.

Thesaurus
'A list of terms authorised to be used in identifying the concepts relevant to a text, together with a statement of the logical or semantic relationships of those terms' [ICA/ADP, p. 27].

Title page
A *macro description* which takes the form of separate page at the front of (generally an extensive) *finding aid*, carrying introductory information. See also *title page section*.

Title page section
A *macro description* using the *title page* model but which is too extensive to be contained on the title page itself. Where this happens, the title page is followed by one or more further pages of explanatory material, giving the background, context and provenance of the materials the *micro descriptions* of which follow. See Section 6.7.

Topical guide
A *guide* which covers archival sources selected to illustrate a topic.

Transfer list
In records management, *lists* of records transferred from current systems to the control of the records management or *archives service*.

Uniform title
In *AACR2*, the title of a bibliographic item which has been chosen to represent all variants titles of the same work. In *MAD*, the concept should be used to indicate that an authority list exists, and has been used to supply a title or name in an archival description.

User
Any person seeking information from archival materials, whether a staff member, an employee of the archive-creating agency, or a member of the public.

Vocabulary
Generally, the terms permitted to be used, or actually used, in an *information retrieval* system or an *index*.

Sources used in the dictionary

Anglo-American Cataloguing Rules, 2nd edition. Gorman, M. & Winkler P. (eds). Library Association, 1978.

ARAD, A. and BELL, L. 'Archival description – a general system', *ADPA* 2 (1978), pp. 2–9.

ARCHIVES OF ONTARIO. *Standardised terminology list*. Task Force on Intellectual Controls, publication no.1, 1988.

BERNER, R. C. *Archival theory and practice in the United States: a historical analysis*, University of Washington Press, Seattle and London, 1983.

BUREAU OF CANADIAN ARCHIVISTS. *Towards descriptive standards*, Ottawa, 1985.

DELMAS, B. *et al.* (eds). *Vocabulaire des archives*, Archivistique et diplomatique contemporaines. Les dossiers de la normalisation AFNOR, Paris, 1986.

EVANS, F. B. *et al.* (comps). 'A basic glossary for archivists, manuscript curators and records managers', *The American Archivist* 37 (1974), 415–33.

GRACY, D. B. *Archives and manuscripts: arrangement and description*, Society of American Archivists, Basic Manual series, Chicago, 1977.

HENSEN, S. L. *Archives, personal papers and manuscripts: a cataloging manual for archive repositories, historical societies and manuscript libraries*, 2nd edition, SAA, Chicago, 1989.

HILDESHEIMER, F. *Guidelines for the preparation of general guides to national archives: a RAMP study*, Unesco, General Information Programme and UNISIST, Paris, 1983.

HOLBERT, S. E. *Archives and manuscripts: reference and access*, Society of American Archivists, Basic Manual series, Chicago, 1977.

HUDSON, J. P. *Manuscript indexing*, British Library, 1979.

INTERNATIONAL COUNCIL ON ARCHIVES, ADP COMMITTEE, *Elementary terms in archival automation*, Koblenz, 1983.

INTERNATION COUNCIL ON ARCHIVES. *Dictionary of Archival Terminology*, Evans, F. B., Himly, F. J. and Walne, P., (comps). ICA handbooks series vol. 3, K. G. Saur, Munich, 1984.

INTERNATIONAL FEDERATION OF LIBRARY ASSOCIATIONS AND INSTITUTIONS *ISBD(NBM): international standard bibliographic description for non-book materials*, IFLA, London, 1977.

JENKINSON, H. *A Manual of archive administration*, 2nd ed. revised, Lund Humphries, London, 1965.

RHOADS, J. B. *The role of archives and records management in national information systems: a RAMP study*, Unesco, Paris, 1983.

ROBINSON, D. (ed). *The listing of archival records*. Proceedings of a Society of Archivists in-service training course held at the Wellcome Institute for the History of Medicine, London, 26–28 March 1985, Society of Archivists, Training Committee, 1986.

ROPER, M. 'The academic use of archives', *Proceedings of the 9th International congress on Archives, London, 15–19 Sept. 1980, Archivum* 29 (1982), pp. 27–45.

SOCIETY OF AMERICAN ARCHIVISTS, NATIONAL INFORMATION SYSTEMS TASK FORCE. *Data elements used in archives, manuscripts, and records repository information.*

SOCIETY OF ARCHIVISTS, *The preparation of finding aids*, Stitt, F. B., (comp), Wolsey Hall, Oxford, 1982.

TAYLOR, H. A. *The arrangement and description of archival materials*, ICA handbooks series vol. 2, K. G. Saur, Munich, 1980.

WALNE, P., *Dictionary of archival terminology*, K. G. Saur, Munich, 1984.

Brief bibliography

This list of works referred to in the course of constructing *MAD2* is restricted to those most immediately relevant or affected. A full bibliography of works in the literature on archival description is expected to appear in associated publications.

Anglo-American cataloguing rules, 2nd edition, Gorman, M. and Winkler, P. W. (eds), Library Association, 1978.

BUREAU OF CANADIAN ARCHIVISTS. *Toward descriptive standards: a report and recommendations of the Canadian working group on archival descriptive standards*, Ottawa, 1985.

BUREAU OF CANADIAN ARCHIVISTS, report of working group on description at fonds level, to the Planning Committee on descriptive standards, March 1988.

DRYDEN, J. E. and HAWORTH, K. M. *Developing descriptive standards: a call to action*, Bureau of Canadian Archivists, Ottawa, 1987.

GRACY, D. B., II. *Archives and manuscripts: arrangement and description*. Basic Manuals series, Society of American Archivists, Chicago, 1977.

HENSEN, S.L. *Archives, personal papers and manuscripts: a cataloging manual for archival repositories, historical societies and manuscripts libraries*, 2nd edition, Society of American Archivists, Chicago, 1989.

HILDESHEIMER, F. *Guidelines for preparation of general guides to national archives: a RAMP study*, Unesco, Paris, 1983.

HOLBERT, S. E. *Archives and manuscripts: reference and access*. Basic Manuals series, Society of American Archivists, Chicago, 1977.

HUDSON, J. P. *Manuscripts indexing*, British Library, 1979.

INTERNATIONAL COUNCIL ON ARCHIVES. *Dictionary of archival terminology*, Evans, B., Himley, F. J. and Walne, P. (eds), ICA Handbooks, Vol 3, K. G. Saur, Munich, 1984.

INTERNATIONAL FEDERATION OF LIBRARY ASSOCIATIONS AND INSTITUTIONS (IFLA). *International standard bibliographical descriptions*, IFLA, London, from 1977.

Invitational meeting of experts on descriptive standards. Working documents and position papers. Ottawa, 4–7 October 1988.

RHOADS, J. B. *The applicability of UNISIST guidelines and ISO international standards to archive administration and records management: a RAMP study*, Unesco, Paris, 1982.

SOCIETY OF AMERICAN ARCHIVISTS, NATIONAL INFORMATION SYSTEMS TASK FORCE. Data

272

elements used in archives, manuscripts, and records repository information systems: a dictionary of standard terminology, In: SAHLI, N., *MARC for archives and manuscripts: the AMC format*, SAA, Chicago, 1985.

SOCIETY OF ARCHIVISTS, TRAINING COMMITTEE. *The listing of archival records*, TR C1, 1986.

TAYLOR, H. A. *The arrangement and description of archival materials*, ICA Handbooks, Vol 2, K. G. Saur, Munich, 1980.

Index